theatre & laughter

Theatre &
Series Editors: Jen Harvie and Dan Rebellato

Theatre&
Series Standing Order ISBN 978–0–230–20327–3

You can receive future titles in this series as they are published by placing a standing order. Please contact your bookseller or, in case of difficulty, write to us at the address below with your name and address, the title of the series and the ISBN quoted above.

Customer Services Department, Macmillan Distribution Ltd, Houndmills, Basingstoke, Hampshire, RG21 6XS, UK

theatre &
laughter

Eric Weitz

macmillan education · palgrave

First published 2016 by
PALGRAVE

Palgrave in the UK is an imprint of Macmillan Publishers Limited, registered in England, company number 785998, of 4 Crinan Street, London, N1 9XW.

Palgrave Macmillan in the US is a division of St Martin's Press LLC, 175 Fifth Avenue, New York, NY 10010.

Palgrave is a global imprint of the above companies and is represented throughout the world.

Palgrave® and Macmillan® are registered trademarks in the United States, the United Kingdom, Europe and other countries.

ISBN 978–1–137–35608–6

This book is printed on paper suitable for recycling and made from fully managed and sustained forest sources. Logging, pulping and manufacturing processes are expected to conform to the environmental regulations of the country of origin.

A catalogue record for this book is available from the British Library.

A catalog record for this book is available from the Library of Congress.

Printed in China

contents

series editors' preface

The theatre is everywhere, from entertainment districts to the fringes, from the rituals of government to the ceremony of the courtroom, from the spectacle of the sporting arena to the theatres of war. Across these many forms stretches a theatrical continuum through which cultures both assert and question themselves.

Theatre has been around for thousands of years, and the ways we study it have changed decisively. It's no longer enough to limit our attention to the canon of Western dramatic literature. Theatre has taken its place within a broad spectrum of performance, connecting it with the wider forces of ritual and revolt that thread through so many spheres of human culture. In turn, this has helped make connections across disciplines; over the past fifty years, theatre and performance have been deployed as key metaphors and practices with which to rethink gender, economics, war, language, the fine arts, culture and one's sense of self.

Theatre & is a long series of short books which hopes to capture the restless interdisciplinary energy of theatre and performance. Each book explores connections between theatre and some aspect of the wider world, asking how the theatre might illuminate the world and how the world might illuminate the theatre. Each book is written by a leading theatre scholar and represents the cutting edge of critical thinking in the discipline.

We have been mindful, however, that the philosophical and theoretical complexity of much contemporary academic writing can act as a barrier to a wider readership. A key aim for these books is that they should all be readable in one sitting by anyone with a curiosity about the subject. The books are challenging, pugnacious, visionary sometimes and, above all, clear. We hope you enjoy them.

Jen Harvie and Dan Rebellato

theatre & laughter

Partners in social relations

On the surface, a joint study of theatre and laughter would appear to be an estimable challenge, or even a fool's errand: a rollicking audience is certain to have at least one member who won't crack a smile, and no two assemblies of spectators will produce quite the same laugh tracks. In addition, theatre works upon us before it actually begins, and is gone even as it happens, a site of guided interaction amongst bodies, minds and phenomena, immediately dispersing into as many different impressions.

The road to a plan begins with the premise that even if we cannot talk with certainty about what any given instance of laughter in the theatre means, and if we accept that it most certainly means different things for different laughers, different things under different circumstances, and even different things *within* a given instance, humans come to know in their bones that laughter means *something* quite

1

revealing about 'what is going on' in a situation, individually and socially. The central argument of this book will undertake to establish theatre and laughter as bound together in human play, dedicated to bonding, flexibility and the expression of what is on our minds and in our bodies. It is the book's broader contention that laughter, as a ubiquitous and sought-after bodied response, is always worth talking about, especially in light of the double-dip intentionality at work in its partnership with theatre-making.

One of the most salient linkages between theatre and laughter is suggested by an observation from a neuroscientist: 'The necessary stimulus for laughter is not a joke, but another person' (Provine, 2004, 215). The substitution of two key words would make Robert Provine's claim a truism about theatre, but the interlocking quote itself comes at the start of Peter Brook's, *The Empty Space*: 'A man walks across this empty space whilst someone else is watching him, and this is all that is needed for an act of theatre to be engaged' (Brook, 9). By identifying two people as the basic operating units for both theatre and laughter, we are directed towards the space between them and what goes on in it, invisible yet palpable.

This book will fix its analytical gaze upon theatre and laughter and their joint animation at the level of social relations (although, in the name of supplying examples with web links for the reader's viewing, a fair number of video/film sequences are included). It will begin with some introductory attention to both subjects and their orientations in human play, before wading in a bit further to the areas of laughter and humour theory. The study begins in earnest with a look at farce as the mother of all genres for laugh-seeking performance, and then proceeds to the comic body bestowed upon western theatre practice by the *commedia dell'arte*. The discussion then proceeds to various areas relevant to laughter and joking in the theatre and beyond, with close attention to the conception and embodiment of these activities. It then goes on to consider representations of laughter, the radical importance of context to the humour transaction, and an ethics of joking. Finally, it will engage with the perpetual debate on laughter in the theatre and its capacity to play a part in urging social change, by examining a salient case in the era of live performance and ever-widening internet audiences.

Laughter and theatre

Which came first, then, theatre or laughter?

Laughter, of course. A line of evolutionary thought contends that laughter developed as a biologically beneficial response prior to speech, a species-wide call of, 'False alarm', to demobilise fight-or-flight tensing for the individual and group. The dramatic loosening of bodied control and the surrender to relaxed breathing returned early humans to a state that prevented them from exhausting reserves of psychic and physical energy needlessly. The open-throated broadcast that meant, 'All clear!' was unmistakable. Its contagiousness came to ensure that the message circulated quickly amongst the group, perhaps averting the unnecessary injury risked by a hair-trigger response from someone thinking that safety was under immediate threat.

Closer to home, so to speak, laughter has been identified as a key bonding response for infant and caregiver. Judith Kay Nelson, a psychotherapist and lecturer in Clinical Social Work, characterises laughter as an 'attachment behaviour'. Whereas crying comes pre-installed at birth, laughter arrives at about three or four months of age; crying signals 'negative arousal', a lack or need of something, while laughter's 'positive arousal' solicits a continuation of desirable attention ('Do it more!'). Think of the face-to-laughing-face exchange between infant and parent/caregiver, bodied expressions of pleasure feeding upon one another in mutual reward.

Tickling is seen as a first step towards the provocation of laughter in another person – what we might as well call humour – in both evolutionary and developmental contexts. Psychoanalytic theorist Adam Phillips, in his short essay on tickling, calls attention both to its pleasurable aspect and to the fact that this pleasure relies on another person for its trigger: 'The child who will be able to feed himself, the child who will masturbate, will never be able to tickle himself. It is the pleasure he cannot reproduce in the absence of the other' (Phillips, 1). Phillips goes on to emphasise the importance of 'shared knowledge' between child and grownup, the precise and secret locations of those sensitive spots in which one is ticklish. As we will come to see, shared, unspoken knowledge is always the active ingredient in 'getting the joke' and the in-group bonding it mobilises, pointing the way towards more complex social operations by the time we arrive at the prospect of tickling a group of spectators through dramatic performance.

Assuming laughter did indeed come first, could theatre have been far behind, especially if we think of it in prototypical terms of intentional enactment? It could not, then, have been long before laughter and theatre found one another. Perhaps some prehistoric, high-functioning primate who was stalking the group's evening meal and, tripped up by a stone in his path, noisily and unceremoniously devolved into a heap on the ground, thereby scaring off the prey. How long did it take for one of his hunting party to simulate this prehistoric pratfall later that day, perhaps indulging in a spirit of well-being amongst the group following eventual triumph – to which the ensuing laughter attested both to positive affect and social bonding?

Although we associate the beginnings of western theatre as we know it with the rise of tragedy in ancient Greece, the cultural practices that led to comedy's formal appearance in 486 BC were already part of the culture. Chief among these was the *kōmos* – from which comedy may have derived its name – a roving rite of revelry in the spirit of Dionysus, god of ecstasy, proponent of wine-drinking, and, as it happens, sponsor of the theatre at which the plays were first performed. The *kōmos*, for classical scholar Stephen Halliwell, was an exuberant surrender to impulses of all kinds, which psychologically provided 'a kind of temporarily induced protection, against the most pressing burdens of life' (Halliwell, 2008, 106). As I will proceed to argue, the capacity to take life, experience and an immediate situation *not* seriously is far from a stain on our collective reputations, but, rather, is a vital feature of human being and a saving grace for the species.

Play's the thing

The behavioural mode that allows us to make the world do what we want, so to speak, is called 'play'. In play, we set aside or otherwise redefine actual circumstances and their everyday meanings. We choose at least for the moment (if not longer, in childhood, sports and theatre) to transpose what we might say we are 'really' doing or talking about to some imagined or alternative context. I may be sitting in a chair in my office, tossing a crumpled piece of paper towards the trash bin across the room, but for the moment I am launching a half-court shot at the buzzer to win the NBA title, while simultaneously supplying ecstatic, incredulous television commentary. I ask my students if they have heard the one about the zombie who walked into a bar, and they know not to expect a factual account. These everyday manifestations of play are open to complex and elaborate variation, both in spontaneous diversions and socially elaborated pastimes.

Twentieth-century sociologist Erving Goffman provides a useful anchor for concepts of play, theatre and laughter in his concept of 'framing', in fact, adopting theatrical terms like 'role' and 'actor' for his own use. We come to internalise a labyrinthine system of situational guidelines with which we navigate daily life, usually knowing without thinking the range of conduct expected, allowed and forbidden in any given situation, from walking amongst strangers on a busy street to rubbing shoulders with the boss at a company function or hosting a holiday dinner for the family. We sometimes duck out of these primary frameworks to indulge in non-serious exchanges that bracket real-life contexts; other times – in the theatre, for example – we enter more purposefully into fictional worlds and alternative circumstances.

Theatre and laughter present themselves as natural soulmates, born of a mutual rooting in this behavioural mode of play. From amongst a range of approaches and disciplines, Brian Sutton-Smith lays out seven 'rhetorics' of play, broad theoretical conceits about its ambiguous nature and purpose. They include a *rhetoric of play as progress*, which applies to the young in human and other species, and helps them prepare in various ways for grown-up life. The *rhetoric of play as the imaginary* refers to its exercise of creativity, invention and fancy; and the *rhetoric of play as frivolous* alludes to its wilful suspension of order and work as our psychic masters. Needless to say, these three concepts have relevance for our meditations on theatre and laughter.

In Trevor Griffiths' *Comedians*, Eddie Waters is a 'favorite comic of yesteryear' convening an evening class for would-be stand-up comedians in a Manchester school classroom. As a warm-up for the evening's performance in front of an agency scout, he sends his charges through several exercises intended to get their creative juices flowing. One round starts with Waters tossing out the word, 'Willy', for improvised quipping:

> PHIL Willy Nilly.
> GED Willy Won'ty.
> PRICE Willy Nocomebackagain.
> CONNOR Willy Ell. (Griffiths, 16)

Waters' exercise stages an episode of managed play for grown-ups, tapping into all three of the above functions it has been claimed to serve. The game, the likes of which might be found in an acting class or boardroom creativity workshop, marks a time out from goal-oriented structures for the encouragement of spontaneity, creativity and group synergy. All these elements are associated with laughter, as well, upon which it might be useful to cast some further introductory light.

Laughter and its double

If theatre constitutes an act of communal playing, laughter is one of its elemental sounds. Scientists tell us that laughter is part of our animal natures, found in near-human primates like chimpanzees, with something like it identified in laboratory rats (which experimenters somehow found ways to tickle). It is a combination of our abilities to multitask intellectually and the structural change that allowed us to walk upright on two legs that ultimately differentiates our laughters from the chimps'.

Neuroscientists distinguish between two types of laughter: Duchenne laughter – named after the nineteenth-century French neurologist who identified it – is considered an involuntary response to an outside stimulus, often humorous or joking intent, and fully involves facial muscles around the mouth and eyes; non-Duchenne laughter involves strategic or pseudo-spontaneous simulation of the response on behalf of a person as social agent. It seems that we laugh more when we are doing the talking than when we are doing the listening, and less at identifiable joking efforts than other kinds of responses or communications. A few moments' reflection should lead one to the realisation that laughters can vary quite a bit in terms of tone and degree, and that a laughter can be spontaneously instigated and still undergo enhancement or modulation for conscious or semi-conscious effect.

Samuel Beckett knew something about theatre and laughter, especially its embodied ironies. As Manfred Pfister points out, while Beckett never bothered to set down a theory of laughter – beyond pithy enumeration of 'the bitter, the hollow and the mirthless' laughs in *Watt* – he gave us dramatic structures littered with embodied thought experiments lying in wait for each individual production. For Beckett, the human body tends to constitute a heartless joke played on each and every one of us, and amongst his dramatic interrogations of the laughing subject lies an interesting assertion in *Waiting for Godot* (1953), leaving room in the argument for us to weigh in through production choices. Vladimir's brief rumination on Christ's crucifixion leads to the subject of repentance, giving way to a 'hearty laugh', which he immediately has to stifle due to his chronic urinary issues:

> VLADIMIR One daren't even laugh any more.
> ESTRAGON Dreadful privation.
> VLADIMIR Merely smile. (*He smiles suddenly from ear to ear, keeps smiling, ceases suddenly.*) It's not the same thing. ... (Beckett, 13)

Vladimir's spontaneous experiment is poised to demonstrate something about genuine feeling and comic effect. If the actor playing Vladimir is able to generate a quality Duchenne smile, its sudden cessation might well be perceived as laughable, in that we know in our bodies that strong feeling cannot be turned off like a light switch. If Vladimir visibly fails to involve his eye muscles in the smile, another, perhaps more cynical reading might ensue. And, of course, many other possibilities.

Vladimir concludes (admits, discovers, etc.) that a laugh is 'not the same thing' as a smile, suggesting he may know a thing or two about evolutionary science. Although we take them to be implicated in one another, humour scholar John Morreall cites research that would have had them separated at birth, tying the smile to the originally defensive 'silent bared-teeth' face, which has come to suggest deference, sympathy and general non-hostility; while the open-mouth 'play face', with its vocalised call, signals a playful state and trust relationship.

Fuzziness ensues when we acknowledge that all of a person's laughters are not the same, neither by degree nor quality. For example, religion scholar Conrad Hyers recounts six classifications in a sort of Beaufort scale for laughter from fourth-century Indian Buddhist thought:

> The descending scale of categories itself suggests that the fullest and most pronounced and enjoyable forms of laughter are at the furthest remove from both piety and propriety: *sita*, a faint, almost imperceptible smile manifest in the subtleties of

facial expression and countenance alone; *hasita*, a smile involving a slight movement of the lips, and barely revealing the tips of the teeth; *vihasita*, a broad smile accompanied by a modicum of laughter; *upahasita*, accentuated laughter, louder in volume, associated with movements of the head, shoulders and arms; *apahasita*, loud laughter that brings tears; and *atihasita*, the most boisterous, uproarious laughter attended by movements of the entire body (e.g., doubling over in raucous guffawing, convulsions, knee-slapping, and hysterics, 'rolling in the aisles'). (Hyers, 33)

Hyers suggests that for some thought systems these broad steps from sedate amusement to mirthful hysteria represent a graded descent from dignity. There is no doubt that a body in spasmodic free fall threatens the constancy of the social fabric, and it should not be surprising that Church and State have had a long and rocky relationship with laughter, both for its uncharitable rumblings and its disruptive, open-bodied physical display. What draws attention away from the response itself, however, is the process by which we seem to be able to pluck it from one another's bodies for better and worse – an initiative we generally call humour or joking.

Killing the frog

Precisely how a humorous utterance causes laughter has been the subject of serious thought going back a few thousand years, with such an aim sometimes decried as a crime against the ineffable beauty of a good joke. An oft misrepresented quote from essayist E.B. White proposes that, 'Humor can be dissected, as a frog can, but the thing dies in the process and the innards are discouraging to any but the pure scientific mind' (White, 243). It is, however, precisely the part of 'getting' a joke from that which resists description which makes it so important to take the poor thing apart, especially in light of the extraordinary effect it has upon the laugher.

Much of the thought about how to cause laughter in one another gravitates towards one or more of the three classic humour theories: the Incongruity Theory proposes generally that laughter is caused by perception of a clash between incompatible ideas or images; the Superiority Theory claims that laughter is brought about by a spontaneous validation of higher status with regard to some joking target; and the Relief Theory suggests that laughter derives from psychic or social tension suddenly defused, demobilised or otherwise released. Senses of surprise, liberation and nonseriousness itself have also been implicated in the incitement of laughter, and other variations or angles have emerged from the interdisciplinary environs of humour studies over the past 40 years. What becomes apparent is how much of laughter's multi-functional nature evades totalising explanation in concrete terms.

The three theories persist, however, as a traditional starting point for talking about humour, and arguably highlight useful intellectual, emotional and psychical elements of what happens when one person makes another person laugh. It would, in fact, seem necessary to include the contributions of all three theories in the mix for a model of humour meant to be in any way comprehensive – and still, any given instance of humour into laughter is the result of an endless snarl of contextual specifics.

Incongruity

Ambiguity, one discovers, remains an operational constant in being human. Languages tend to generate words that sound the same and mean decidedly different things. The winning joke from the Edinburgh Fringe Festival a few years ago, went, 'I needed a password eight characters long, so I picked Snow White and the Seven Dwarves' – a cute confection exposing irreconcilable meanings of a single, commonly used word ('character') and, by inference, the inefficiencies of language, our most revered tool for communication.

In the embodied terms of theatre and performance, dialogue and enactment can be made to cast amusing shadows upon one another. Lady Augusta Gregory's short farce, *Spreading the News* (1904), centres upon misapprehended utterances and runaway gossip in a rural Irish village, which has Bartley Fallon, the most unlikely of townspeople, perceived as a hayfork-wielding murderer. An overweening provincial magistrate and a local policeman spot the suspect onstage, with the former calling attention to his 'guilty look', before concluding, 'He must have found escape difficult – he is trying to brazen it out' (Gregory, 323). Gregory's text provides ample opportunity to frame a laughable disjunction between the 'guilty look' of a homi-cidal adulterer as perceived by the gossiping villagers, and the scripted sad sack as might be embodied in production (I tend to imagine Bartley as a Woody Allen type or a human incarnation of Eeyore).

Much of the scholarly thinking about how to make peo-ple laugh now accepts some variation on the concept of incongruity – called variously frame clash, script switch, error detection and other things. Humour scholar John Morreall includes in the critical lineage of the Incongruity Theory Immanuel Kant, Sören Kierkegaard and Arthur Schopenhauer, the last of whom proposed: 'The cause of laughter in every case is simply the sudden perception of the incongruity between a concept and the real objects which have been thought through it in some relation, and laughter itself is just the expression of this incongruity' (Morreall, 1987, 52). Morreall's own contribution contends that, 'The playful enjoyment of a cognitive shift is expressed in laugh-ter' (Morreall, 2009, 49). In the Snow White joke above, the cognitive shift comes about through a play on 'charac-ter', swapping the mundane chore of inventing unhackable passwords with a frivolous image from a Disney classic.

The linguistics-based General Theory of Verbal Humor (GTVH), advanced by Salvatore Attardo and Victor Raskin (1991), goes a long way towards elaborating an incongruity-resolution approach that accounts for target, context and delivery. It identifies six 'knowledge resources' deemed essential to the workings of a joke. Chief among them is the Script Opposition, essentially a variation on the concept of incongruity, with 'script' a specialist usage that refers to stereotypical information about people, places and practices, carried in our cultural storehouse of knowledge. Attardo presents for sample analysis the joke, 'What do you get when you cross a *mafioso* with a postmodern theorist? Someone who will make you an offer you cannot understand' (Attardo, 2008, 109). The second line is immediately recognisable from the pop-culture *mafioso* script (courtesy of *The Godfather*). The (il)logical switch at the very last word from the expected 'refuse' to 'understand' owes, of course, to a postmodern-theorist script that includes a reputation for impenetrable theory. One might foresee how this linguistics-based model could be extrapolated for a theory of dramatic discourse and/or comic performance by refashioning or augmenting the resources to account for extra-linguistic elements like vocal registers, physical 'languages' and embodied scripts.

We should note the element of alternative sense-making required in connecting the incompatible frames, or as linguist Wallace Chafe calls it, 'pseudo-plausibility', without which the joke lapses into mere nonsense and/or risks a response of, 'I don't get it'.

Superiority

Viewers of *The Simpsons* will be familiar with Nelson Muntz, the archetypal schoolyard bully, who rarely misses a chance to spotlight another character's misfortune with a trademark, 'Ha-ha!'. His pressed, singsong delivery, accompanied by a pointing finger, singles out laughter's derisive edge for emphasis, perhaps echoing many a ten-year-old's first flush of infatuation with triumphalism. Plato and Aristotle pronounced – perceptively, if disapprovingly – upon the element of ridicule found in laughter. Seventeenth-century thinker Thomas Hobbes coined the catch phrase for the Superiority Theory of humour, the feeling of 'sudden glory' over another person or one's former self, embodied all too self-servingly by laughter.

There is undoubtedly something distasteful to Nelson's *gestus* of disparagement, which might explain why elements of society have periodically attempted to steer our comic ideals towards a more genteel or 'benign' humour, as in the eighteenth century's 'sentimental' comedies. In 'An Essay on Comedy', written in 1877, George Meredith characterises a kind of preferred humour that elicits amusement but means no harm: 'You may estimate your capacity for comic perception by being able to detect the ridicule of them you love without loving them less; and more by being able to see yourself somewhat ridiculous in dear eyes, and accepting the correction their image of you proposes' (Meredith, 42).

Thirteen years later, Henri Bergson acknowledged the more traditional, perhaps inescapable, opposing view, very much in the air in this, the age of the Epic Fail. In his essay on 'Laughter' (*'Le Rire'*, 1900), Bergson proposes: 'Laughter is, above all, a corrective. Being intended to humiliate, it must make a painful impression on the person against whom it is directed. By laughter, society avenges itself for the liberties taken with it. It would fail in its object if it bore the stamp of sympathy or kindness' (Bergson, 1980, 187). More recently, sociologist Michael Billig bids us drop the pretensions about humorous laughter's positive good works and acknowledge it unapologetically for the correctional cudgel it is. Billig marshals thought by Bergson and Sigmund Freud as the basis for his approach: 'It suggests that ridicule lies at the core of social life, for the possibility of ridicule ensures that members of society routinely comply with the customs and habits of their social milieu' (Billig, 2). This calls attention to the idea that all jokes are made at someone's or something's expense, even if the butt is so widely accepted or seemingly ineffectual as to seem invisible (such as the Snow White joke, above).

We may indeed have occasion to experience amusement in which ridicule operates as a recessive element at most, such as silliness or absurdity (evoking Freud's childlike humour as distinguished from the tendentious joking of adulthood), and the bonding aspect of laughter can sometimes be enough to push a group to mirthful distraction. It may be that the concept of superiority narrows the restriction untenably – clearly every joke does not amount to an assertion over another person (or oneself, formerly). It is, though, hard to ignore the sense of personal or subjective validation that gives many a belly laugh its bursting edge, particularly evident in political joking and the comic comeuppance suffered by humourless characters in dramatic scenarios. Parody, as imitation plus critique, and satire, as comedy with outrage in the ascendant, remain popular vessels for humorous intent that feature the aggressive impulse in contemporary laughter provocation.

Relief

Morreall reports that body-based approaches to laughter gathered loosely under the banner of Relief Theory arose in the eighteenth century, alongside the Incongruity Theory: 'So in the first versions of the Relief Theory, the nervous system was represented as a network of tubes inside which the animal spirits sometimes build up pressure, as in emotional excitement, that calls for release' (Morreall, 2009, 16). Lord Shaftesbury, Herbert Spencer and John Dewey top the historical roster of relief theorists, although Freud tends to receive most of the attention. He attributes to laughter a particular function of releasing energy built up from the mobilisation of psychic effort to repress socially unacceptable sexual and aggressive urges. Freud appears most impressed with the laughter derived from a category he delineates as humour, capable of transmuting the rising affect caused by impending emotional distress into a pleasurable discharge.

To whatever extent one accepts Freud's detailed explanations of psycho-physical hydraulics, it is hard not to acknowledge some notion of cathartic effect in laughter's full-bodied, full-throated release and its subsequent denouement. Ultimately, Freud's output on jokes and humour contains thought that would associate him at different times with all three camps, supporting the proposition that the theories represent jointly useful approaches to any grand apprehension of humorous laughter.

Other angles

From a cognitive and evolutionary perspective Matthew M. Hurley, Daniel C. Dennett and Reginald B. Adams, Jr., contend collectively that our adaptive biologies have supplied us with bursts of pleasurable affect for suddenly, that is, 'just in time', discovering a mistaken or ill-advised conviction. In the beginning, this was designed to preserve our safety by making it feel good to avoid jumping to conclusions, but we have come to seek stimulus of the response in primarily non-threatening situations because we like it. Humorous laughter persists as a mechanism for rewarding us upon daily recognition of 'false belief' – joking generally trades on leading us down one path, to find ourselves ambushed by another – thereby encouraging us away from exceeding rigidity and/or security in all we think we know.

According to Chafe, the spectacle that a laughing body makes of itself is doubly functional: it temporarily prevents the laugher from undertaking serious thought and activity by interfering with breathing and bodied cohesion; at the same time it generates unmistakable visual and vocal signals that such a state has been adopted by a member of the group: 'Also of crucial importance is the fact that this emotional state is a pleasant one – pleasant enough to be psychologically as well as physically distracting. The result is that the feeling of nonseriousness keeps us from either acting or thinking in a serious way' (Chafe, 23). This approach might be seen as related to the Relief Theory until one thinks of it not simply as a time out from serious mode, but a beneficial way of being in its own right.

Embodied joking

We do not have to commit to a unifying theory of theatre and laughter to acknowledge that human play represents the psychic soil for their flourishing. Let us, in any case, finally have a look in detail at that confluence between embodied theatre practice and a clearly marked attempt to evoke laughter. From the oceans of possible examples comes the opening of a priceless comic monologue, titled, 'Giving Notes', written by Victoria Wood for a BBC programme in 1985 (*As Seen on TV*). This piece, potentially viewable at http://www.youtube.com/watch?v=1qK80wVXZ9w, allows us to look at the scripted lines and its original performance by Julie Walters in front of a studio audience. It draws upon theatre-related experience for its comic traction.

The monologue amounts to a note-giving session conducted by the director of an amateur theatre group, described as 'a middle-aged sprightly woman':

> ALMA Right. Bit of hush please. Connie! Thank you. Now that was quite a good rehearsal; I was quite pleased. There were a few raised eyebrows when we let it slip the Piecrust Players were having a bash at Shakespeare but I think we're getting there. But I can't say this too often; it may be *Hamlet* but it's got to be Fun Fun Fun! (Wood, 1995)

As written, the first few lines evoke the atmosphere following a rehearsal run-through, replete with chattering cast and encouraging director. The homiest of company names and the jaunty proposition of 'having a bash' at the most revered of western playwrights sidle towards levity in what might be considered a comic priming sequence in the first few lines.

Even prior to Walters' characterisation the voice as written suggests softly brandished authority, a pointedly folksy register that already rings bells for anyone who has spent time with a local theatre company. The last line above, then, displays the classic construction of a joke in a dramatic context. The preface, 'But I can't say this too often', supplies a running start to the setup, 'it may be *Hamlet* …'. The play's title may already look out of place in the amateur-drama context. The image summoned by *Hamlet* – widely perceived as the Everest of theatrical aspiration – is then upended by the exhortation to have 'Fun Fun Fun', a conversational cliché representing social character and conceptual approach risibly at odds with a play generally considered synonymous with something like the most serious, lofty and daunting theatre piece a company can tackle.

The reversal opens a gap within which shared, unspoken meaning and critique beckon approval through audience laughter. By forcing the *Hamlet* frame up against the 'Fun Fun Fun' frame, the utterance deftly mines everyday knowledge from these seemingly incompatible strips of experience. One can never talk confidently about the spur to a given person's laughter, but this joke stands to make fun of excess in both directions: on one hand towards the po-faced reverence accorded Shakespeare in general and his best-known tragedy in particular; on the other towards a social type found here and there, including local theatre groups, with a parochial, compulsively sunny outlook and all it entails for a philosophy of theatre-making. (And maybe even an extra slice of pleasure for survivors of 'professional' theatre, the pressures and pragmatics of which can tend to extinguish some of that fun fun fun.) The fact that it has accomplished all this with astounding efficiency is considered one of the keys to its stimulation of the laughter response – and the reason we are accused of 'killing the frog' by taking apart the 'Aha' moment in such dry, methodical terms.

Having gone some way towards parsing the joke through its verbal traces on the page, it is interesting to look at the comic value added by Walters in performance. At first sight and in the first few lines, her embodiment conjures a cultural 'type' inflected for comedy through measured emphasis on costume, carriage and vocal mannerism. For the first big laugh line, analysed above, she efficiently quiets the gathered cast, then launches into the opening remarks about the 'few raised eyebrows' with which her selection of Shakespeare was met, including provisional praise about the progress being made. With the words, 'But I can't say this too often' – and to an extent that cannot be inferred by the mere words of a script – Walters downshifts the tone towards genuinely felt, long-held conviction. The temptation might be to colour the line with the compulsive optimism the words suggest, but Walters' unembellished, impassioned delivery lends weight to the utterance. Allowing a fervent shrillness to creep into her voice for, 'Fun Fun Fun', emphasises the disjunction between the feel-good philosophy in the words and the earnest demonstration of commitment in the performing body, thereby incarnating the frame clash.

Good comic writing creates spaces for good comic acting and Bergson's essay harbours useful pointers for comic performers in this regard. His contention that a *'comic effect is always obtainable by transposing the natural expression of an idea into another key'* (140), goes some way towards describing the embodied strategy that underpins Walters' performance. Each new note to a cast member sees a behavioural adjustment recognisable from an array of registers relevant to the stage-director context, yet calculated to send the verbal instruction into comic relief vis-à-vis the monumental theatrical endeavour represented by *Hamlet*, its well-known characters and scenes.

In a later passage Walters has just admonished the actor playing Ophelia for diverging from Shakespeare's text in the mad scene (approximately the 0:40 time mark). Walters continues, talking directly to the offending actor imagined to be somewhere out in the audience, reminding her that, 'this is our marvellous bard, Barbara, you cannot paraphrase'. Taking a slight pause as she returns to her notepad and flipping a few pages, Walters appears to have reassigned her focus to finding the next note as, like an afterthought, she explains, 'It's not like Pinter where you can more or less say what you like as long as you leave enough gaps'.

In seeming to divert focus from the words being said (what we sometimes call a 'throwaway' delivery), the implied dramaturgical critique of another English playwright's style – in particular, his perceived affectation regarding scripted pauses – emerges as a rote voicing of a theatrical given, thereby sharpening the joke's edge.

Subsequent audiences

These ruminations address the workings of the laughter trap in impossibly general terms and, inescapably, from the perspective of a single viewer. As I have emphasised, humorous laughter is rooted in the who-what-where-when of the here and now, endlessly beholden to contextual details, some of which connect synchronously to social and cultural circuitries, also wired to timeworn performance practices and humour patterns.

And so 'Giving Notes' also lends itself to discussion of the sort of routine problematisation invited by any text that would seek out laughter on more than a highly localised, one-time-only basis. In the late (which is to say, numerically lower) 400s, BC, Aristophanes had the luxury of writing for an audience of adult Athenian males with a fairly circumscribed and knowable realm of social awareness. As the Hellenic sphere opened up towards the end of the next century and comedy required mobility, dramatic humour had to make itself available to a broader reach of experience. For this and other reasons, it could no longer rely on specific, locally known targets – it began to present 'types' of people and common life events for comic construction, substantially expanding the joking catchment areas. In the formative era of western comic practice, Renaissance Italy's *commedia dell'arte* generated a flexible roster of character types or 'masks', thereby preying upon a seemingly undying predilection by cultures to stereotype inhabitants of their own geographical regions.

This brief detour comes by way of acknowledging my own comic connection to 'Giving Notes', despite my indirect access to the ground zero of its original referents. Having received most of my theatre grounding in the United States and relocated to Ireland a little over twenty years ago, I think I know pretty much what the sketch is talking about, even if I cannot claim direct experience of Alma as a comic mask born of English cultural knowledge. This, though, is what the comic practitioner is up against, especially in the mainstream, potentially global marketplace. The sketch offers key, broadly available points of contact, even if my personal experience fails to fit perfectly.

In fact, when you laugh at a comic performance from another culture, there is always some element of not really knowing what you are laughing at. More accurately, although you may be able to account for the main triggers of your response, you almost surely lack the kernel of in-group knowledge held by the ground-zero audience. It is far less of a leap, however, to claim that people do laugh in all cultures and that they attempt to *make* each other laugh through recognizable humour-related strategies. Salvatore Attardo summarizes a conviction among many humour scholars, supported by a wave of linguistics-related research in the 1980s, that, 'the mechanisms of humor are universal and transcultural' (Attardo, 1994, 209).

A play like Wole Soyinka's *The Trials of Brother Jero* (1960), born of Nigerian Yoruba culture in the mid-twentieth century, employs a con-artist figure to satirize the power structures primed by religious indoctrination and a sort of interlocking human susceptibility to smooth self-interest. The 'beach prophet', Brother Jeroboam, peddles advice and hope to his devotees. He owes money to Amope for a cape she sold him, a debt he apparently has no intention of paying. We see the shrewish, manipulative manner in which she treats Chume, her husband, as he brings her upon his bicycle to lay siege to her debtor. Without knowing the target of his insufferable wife's attack, Chume, on his own accord, has been petitioning the holy man for divine permission to beat her. ('Just once, Prophet. Just once' (Soyinka, 57).)

The play in soft focus resembles western texts like Molière's *Tartuffe* (1664) and *The Music Man* (1957), with an audience at a theatrical distance urged towards humorous laughter at the brazen ease with which a charlatan robs victims of their money or virtue. Readers or spectators outside the target context of *Brother Jero* would be unfamiliar with Yoruba custom and 'beach prophets'; many people today – from Africa and elsewhere alike – would not consider wife-beating a laughable topic, even with tongue in cheek. The real point to reinforce from this example, is that audiences can laugh (or not) at the same text for different reasons, owing to perceived points of contact from their own up-to-the-minute spheres of reference.

The heart of lightness

Brian Sutton-Smith, to whom we looked for an overview of play theory, ultimately enlists Stephen Jay Gould's evolutionary principles of *quirkiness* and *redundancy*, generated by *flexibility*, to underpin his own *rhetoric of play as adaptive variability*. While the 'quirky shifts' he attributes to play would fit obviously into a discussion of laughter incitement, redundancy proves an interesting partner. Sutton-Smith explains redundancy as the generating of copies once a useful structure has been found, and he offers as examples our abundance of ball games and card games. In this way, dramatic genre could be seen to supply a selection of shells or textual templates for the elaboration of theme, character, plot and, indeed, emotional bearing.

Comedy, laughter's home super-genre, has by definition declined to take the world seriously through its many historical guises, and for its trouble still tends to receive somewhat less respect than tragedy. It has been my own proposition that the comic spirit embodies a human need to take the world playfully for more than escapist purposes, which keeps comedy alive and well, perhaps more sustainably than tragedy. John Morreall goes a step further to suggest that we may have 'outgrown' tragedy from a functionalist perspective. Tragedy is the genre of irresistible emotional force and black-and-white choices; it valorises singularity of mind and heart, perhaps because it was born of a society that placed high value on militaristic virtues. Morreall points out that Sophocles' Antigone seems

27

resolutely to see her options either as burying her brother and taking the consequences, or bowing to Creon's will (by not burying him) and living in unbearable dishonour. The comic sensibility is far more resourceful, he claims, and would have generated many alternatives in Antigone's circumstances: 'The world of tragedy is full of problems that would be quickly solved in comedy, with a little imagination' (Morreall, 2009, 79).

Tragic heroes in all their lion-hearted resolve, Morreall proposes, are presented through comedy in an entirely different light: 'If a person with a locked will or an obsession appears in a comedy, by contrast, it's not as a hero to be admired, but as the butt of joking' (80). Furthermore, Morreall reminds us that comedy 'grew out of fertility rites and ever since has emphasized the basics in human life – food, sex, and getting along with family, friends, and even enemies' (81). He concludes: 'Treating life as a series of battles is now a source of harmful stress. The playful, imaginative attitude fostered by comedy not only feels better, but makes us healthier psychologically and physically' (81).

Regardless of whether one thinks that Morreall makes a case for tragedy to be formally retired, the other kind of generic world we are talking about here leads to the purest of laughter-generating forms: farce persists as the fully loaded generic vehicle comprised of all the bits of dramatic machinery dedicated to causing laughter. Its spirit lies in pure theatrical play; childlike in its zest, yet adult in its appetites. Farcical worlds tend towards typical areas for playful treatment, as described by Jessica Milner Davis,

28

in her seminal study on the subject: 'Farce favors direct, visual, and physical jokes over rich, lyric dialogue (although words are not unimportant in farce and can be crucial to its quarrels, deceptions and misunderstandings), and it declares an open season for aggression, animal high spirits, self-indulgence and rudeness in general' (Davis, 2–3). The farcical body says, 'This is play'; its heavily outlined performative palette supplies the kinds of crisp reversals and energetic charges that both support comic effect and mark the stage world's remove from realistic representation.

With a birthright in the formative dramatic practices of ancient Greece and Rome, contributions from the embodied repertoire of the *commedia dell'arte*, and refinement of a classic recipe on the nineteenth-century Parisian boulevard, farce contains or points to all the laughter-inducing approaches to character, plot and situation we have come to associate with comedy and the comic. Farce wages comic war against pretence, rigidity, and civilised thought cut off from its corporeal basics, as distilled by Davis:

> The fundamental jokes around which a farce-plot turns are probably the inescapable facts that all human dignity is at the mercy of the human body and its appetites and needs; and that those human bodies themselves are imprisoned by the space/time continuum. (3)

Less lofty than tragedy in its aspirations, yet dedicated to its pursuits with the full force of its biological drives, farce's plots are often based on scheming or evasion. There is a kind of laughter one hears in audiences attending classic farces, a sort of explosive bemusement when a character blatantly – and, in performance, earnestly or cavalierly – pours forth statements so diametrically opposed to the truth that it represents a pratfall by the sense of basic honest dealing that we are pleased to consider a cornerstone of civilisation. In a farce by Georges Feydeau, for example – and I'm thinking of *A Flea in Her Ear* (*La Puce à l'oreille*, 1907) – the man-servant's wife, having been glimpsed by her husband in an incriminating position with a strange man at a hotel of questionable repute, has rushed home and into her work clothes seconds before he bursts in to exact an explanation. 'What d'you mean, locking the door like that?' he demands. 'I didn't lock the door', she answers, no doubt as composed an untruth as you can imagine. He goes on to put the question to her, 'The point is, what were you doing ten minutes ago at the Hotel Casablanca?', leading, after as many conversational detours as she can manufacture to the simple (false) statement: 'I haven't left this house'. She proceeds to deny the accusation to the point of suggesting he ring the concierge by way of testimony that she hadn't left the apartment, after which we discover through an aside that she had taken the precaution of bribing the witness in advance.

In classic farce the stakes retain mere domestic and social weight, referring largely to face-saving and, indeed, marriage-saving aims. The departure from truth-saying comes as a sudden matter of urgency, and so it may not only be the blitheness of fabrication that inspires ironic laughter, but the increasing degree of fabulous invention to which the character resorts.

Shadow laughter

The classic comic plot strategy of avoidance, observed in the previous section, contains straightforward lying responses to simple questions, and I believe their potential comic effects are related to a kind of humour found now in hyper-deadly contemporary worlds like those in the television series, *Breaking Bad* (AMC, 2008–13). For me there is a delicious discomfort in each new fabrication told by Walt (Bryan Cranston) to Skyler (Anna Gunn), his wife, in his somehow knockabout descent into high-stakes drug production, treachery and murder. Each new showdown leads to another high-wire improvisation by Walt, and just when you think he might as well come clean, he reaches back for another last-gasp concoction in a spirit of true farcical audacity. Feydeau revealed that his job as a farceur was to engineer situations in which two people who should under no circumstances run into one another, do – a major premise of shows like *Breaking Bad*, *Dexter* (2006–13) and, more recently, *Fargo* (2014–). Any comic highlights in their otherwise pitch-black fabrics derive to some extent from their farcical affinities.

The other side of this modern-day coin derives from a strategy of bald-faced truth-telling in comic worlds. It represents a feature commonly exploited in new-breed American sitcoms. *Modern Family* (2009–), in fact, runs a televisual variation on the old-fashioned theatrical aside by intercutting a character's disingenuous utterance with a living-room rebuttal to the camera. *Arrested Development* (2003–6, 2013) cultivated the art of the after-joke through disattended reactions or mutterings to, for example, almost everything Tobias says regarding his acting aspirations and his barely repressed sexuality.

To rein our discussion back to the stage, Alfred Jarry may have been little more than a rude and cheeky school-boy when he conceived the character who became *Ubu Roi* (1896), but in making travesties of Macbeth and his Lady he was one of the first to show what can happen when farce answers the call of the Dark Side. Bumbling, illogical and succeeding only insofar as dramatic licence commissions each new episode of barbaric silliness, Ubu sets music-hall slapstick (stomping on someone's foot) as a cue to start the revolution and receives mortal wounds only to appear good as new in the next scene. Granted, the range for concretisation in performance remains fairly wide, but this larger-than-life paragon of stupidity and ineptitude (a role Homer Simpson and Peter Griffin have been dying to get their hands on) throws off satiric sparks against God and Country *because* of the comic unworthiness with which, step by pre-posterous step, he somehow keeps rising. It says more about the shoddy workmanship of the surrounding world than the individual on display if a cowardly and self-centred farcical protagonist succeeds continually by embodying the opposite of all cultural ideals.

Almost a century later, Frank McGuinness's 1988 play, *Carthaginians*, shows the two-way comic refraction that the background and foreground of a stage world are capable of generating. Three women maintain a vigil in the Creggan graveyard, 'waiting for the dead to rise', as these and other Derry-born characters grope towards psychic refuge in the long shadow cast by events on Bloody Sunday in 1971. Within a context that has clear ties to classical tragedy, the women trade dirty jokes to pass the time. The first, about a man who has mistaken his penis for a cigar, might score well enough on the stupid-male scale, especially under whatever weight of mood the production has established. The second requires demonstration as to how an Englishwoman, a Frenchwoman and a Derry woman would tend to take on a banana. For this one, the enacted punchline alludes to coerced sex, which might accomplish the very opposite of lightening the mood. These two 'jokes', however, set the stage for a third, told later by Maela:

> A woman walks into a doctor's office and she says, 'Doctor, doctor, I've a pain'. 'Where's the pain?' says the doctor. The woman says, 'In my child, in my child there is a pain. A pain in her heart and in her head and in her hair'. So the doctors shave the child bald and the child dies with no hair. Isn't that a great joke? Isn't it? (McGuinness, 317–18)

Although written at least from the start in a joking register, the story gradually slides into a cruel non-joke, in that it is exactly what happened to her daughter. Certainly in the second and third cases, this is joking turned inside out to emotionally brutal effect. The joke – a short-form narrative mode dedicated to laughter – has been itself reversed upon in ways that expose how mechanical our response to joking form can be.

Later on, Dido, a young man and the only connection to the outside world, has the group act out a play he has written, titled, 'The Burning Balaclava'. The play-within-a-play's tragic events and inflammatory issues are turned all but farcical by its travesty of Irish drama and sectarian convictions. The roles are all cross-cast; production values include a stuffed dog, with squirt guns and religious paraphernalia used as lethal weaponry, and the theme song from *High Noon* played on cassette. McGuinness here has rigged deadly serious material with broadly comic trappings that find their basis in the relative naughtiness of extra-marital playgrounds.

From farce's nineteenth century apotheosis as laughter-centric diversion, the existential zeitgeist and historical horrors of the twentieth century compelled some practitioners to consider it as lit from below. How else to express the seemingly random manipulation of happenstance for maximum misfortune than through the genre of leering nightmare; what more relevant model for the dark arts of anti-communication than farce's natural affinity for deception? The outright laughter for which the stripped-down form gained its popularity appears to teeter between grim irony and defiant truth-telling.

Humour as embodied practice

Before inspecting a recent/current incarnation of the farcical spirit, let us diverge momentarily to recognise the full purchase upon a spectating body gained by humorous utterances that lead to laughter. Without wanting to frighten anyone, we may have to admit that if we drill down to any given instance of consciously caused laughter (whatever else it does) a joke is an attack, a manipulation, an attempt at seduction. A humorous utterance attempts to bring about an internal version of what tickling accomplishes from the outside, a conspicuous response in the receiving body that suggests formidable goings-on within. It is also possible, in less amiable circumstances, that it attempts to stamp upon the listeners their out-group status, if not targeted ridicule. How often have we been on one end or the other of an awkwardly unsuccessful humour bid, followed by a rescue attempt with some form of, 'I was only joking'?

The fact remains that, however unassuming the conscious intent, no one is ever *only* joking. Along with the blatant intention of shaking another person bodily from within comes the veiled thought and feeling which was not to be taken 'seriously'. One need not presume sinister intent on the part of all comically inclined theatre-makers to acknowledge that tangible impact upon the bodies in the theatre is simply what we do. Erin Hurley elaborates an approach to theatre that locates a central element of its appeal in the way that feeling encompasses the spectator bodily, intellectually and imaginatively in a socially situated weave.

She adopts from sociology a concept of 'feeling-labour' to characterise the intentionality of the theatre-maker in, say, embodying the larger-than-life emotions of melodrama: 'By "feeling-labour" I intend to capture the work theatre does in making, managing, and moving feeling in all its types (affect, emotions, moods, sensations) in a publicly observable display that is sold to an audience for a wage' (Hurley, 2010, 9). Comic performance undoubtedly is a prime example of the theatre-maker's designs on our bodied apparatus. By extrapolating to a theatre context a one-to-one joking transaction, humour strategies appear as common tools in the physical, sensate, intellectual and emotional negotiations between stage and auditorium – feeling-labour implicitly undertaken when a theatre-maker sets out to provoke a laughter response from a collection of spectators.

One Man, Two Guvnors (2011) allows us to look at a farce-like text channelled by writer Richard Bean from Carlo Goldoni's eighteenth-century comedy, *The Servant of Two Masters* (*Il servitore di due padroni*, 1753), itself derived from the plots and masks of the *commedia dell'arte*. The original National Theatre production had hugely successful runs in London and New York, with touring still going through the year of this book's publication. It reveals the design of a laughter machine – theatre playing for its own sake – containing genre-defining dramaturgical parts like word play, doubling and mistaken identity, increasingly audacious scheming, and slapstick.

At the same time, however, this production directs our attention to comic practices that mine the actual presence of performer and spectator as parties to the transaction. Several centuries ago the *commedia dell'arte* elaborated the twin engines of laughter provocation in performance: virtuosity and spontaneity. As marketplace entertainment, *commedia* performances had to grab and hold audience attention, and they did so via a customisable assortment of scenarios that allowed for a mix of set routines and guided improvisations. Performers cultivated personalised versions of stock characters or *masks*, based on an array of comedy-friendly prototypes like obdurate old men and mischievous servants. Troupes and their performers carried with them a collection of well-rehearsed set pieces, called *lazzi*, often capable of wowing an audience with physical, vocal or ensemble virtuosity for humorous effect. The performers had licence to surf the waves of laughter, gauging interest and amusement comparable to today's street performers, and shifting from comic detour to plot advancement accordingly.

Born-again strains of *commedia* emerged in the twentieth and twenty-first centuries, with a broad physicality and a comic sensibility dedicated to illuminating the humorous facets of individual behaviour in social situations. Contemporary Italian practitioners like Antonio Fava have attempted to carry the flag for *commedia*'s historical tradition, while other companies, like Ireland's Corn Exchange, have sought to apply its character-based physicality to open up modern texts and issues. As far as theatre and laughter go, there can be no more opportune specimen for observation of *commedia*'s lasting influence on comic performance than *One Man, Two Guvnors*, with its original cast.

Bean's version transposes the scenario of *The Servant of Two Masters* to Brighton, England, at the dawn of the Swinging Sixties. This historical positioning allows for updates of stock *commedia* characters, placing them at a tethered remove, close enough to now, yet laughably then. The scenario, as scripted by Goldoni, provides a string of comic situations through which a down-at-heel serving man must carry out the instructions of his two different employers without letting them find out about one another.

Word play

The range of comic access to the spectating body is as varied as it is familiar, supplying a complement to deep and grandiose emotion as well as a partner in feeling management. At one end of the mind–body continuum, comic contact through the intellect can be enjoined through word play, which is to say, making language or verbal communication the underlying target of amusement. We might say that word play in dramatic performance involves an embodied enshrinement of quick or slow thinking on the part of one or more characters, often through displays of linguistic invention or mishap.

Farce-related embodiment is known for its demands of high energy and virtuosic precision, perhaps contributing to the sensory exhilaration that adds to the charge in the here-and-now of laughter creation. One such sequence in *One Man, Two Guvnors* combines clever scripting with room for tight, double-act playing. Stanley, one of the cast's 'two guv'nors', notices Francis, the 'one man', with a familiar-looking photo. Francis, caught between masters, has invented a friend named Paddy, whom he says received the picture frame from his employer before he died:

> STANLEY Were you there?
> FRANCIS When?
> STANLEY When he was diagnosed with diarrhoea but died of diabetes.
> FRANCIS No, I was in Didcot, and he was diagnosed with diarrhoea but died of diabetes in Dagenham. (73–4)

This is only a portion of the sequence, and it is rendered at a fair clip, similar to vaudeville and music hall custom (you can see it at around the 2:20 mark of the 'Show Clips' link listed in the bibliography). It demands attention to rhythm, crisp articulation *and* a sort of discursive integrity, as the accumulation of 'd' words wrestles with the logical snarl of Francis' tale-spinning, benefitting in comic terms from an increasing momentum that highlights the alliteration and increasingly desperate invention. One false start or trip of the tongue in a given performance and the challenge has failed, like a juggler coming a cropper amidst a clatter of pins. There is a sense, here, of the performers playing for the audience, and part of the laughter surely derives from a thrill of watching players who are really good at it.

Tom Stoppard is one of our most adept purveyors of verbal wit, and *Rosencrantz and Guildenstern Are Dead* (1967) offers word play in a most literal sense. It shows the world of Shakespeare's *Hamlet* from the reverse perspective of two minor characters, embodying interlocking off-stage activities parallel to the Dane's tragic journey. In a Beckettian twilight zone, the title characters pass time between interludes with Hamlet by, among other things, practising a game that requires the two players to improvise conversation for which each new contribution must take the form of a question. The first one to make a statement or otherwise falter concedes a point to the other (and this *is* something you can try at home or in Acting class). It is outfitted by Stoppard in joke-like fashion as a variation on tennis (they 'serve' to begin a game, and the scoring substitutes the word, 'love', for zero) and with debate-like rigour (e.g., 'No *non-sequiturs*', 'No synonyms'). In supplying a quasi-formal gaming structure to his word play, Stoppard sets a challenge for the characters, the actors and himself, leading to passages like this in the first act:

> GUIL What's your name when you're at home?
> ROS What's yours?
> GUIL When I'm at home?
> ROS Is it different at home?
> GUIL What home?
> ROS Haven't you got one?
> GUIL Why do you ask?
> ROS What are you driving at?
> GUIL (*with emphasis*) What's your name?!
> ROS Repetition. Two-love. Match point to me.
> (Stoppard, 35)

The performance by the playwright is notable, not only for its verbal contrivance, but for an ability to enfold into it a vehicle for character exposition: contrary to type, Rosencrantz will manage to best his intellectual better by keeping competitive focus while Guildenstern loses his head to emotion.

Shortly thereafter, the two characters ruminate upon the hurried courtship of Claudius and Gertrude following Hamlet's father's death:

> GUIL Indecent.
> ROS Hasty.
> GUIL Suspicious.
> ROS It makes you think.
> GUIL Don't think I haven't thought of it.
> ROS And with her husband's brother.
> GUIL They were close.
> ROS She went to him –
> GUIL – too close –
> ROS – for comfort. (42)

These patter-like exchanges trifle with words as individual units of meaning, in their clichéd mingling and in coincidental significance beyond the awareness of the characters. Dramatic dalliance with sound, meaning and rhythm would appear to court a certain pleasure at the expense of language and its pretence as the currency with which we carry out our most serious, civilised social interaction.

Slapstick

Whereas word play is a kind of candy for the mind, slapstick can be seen as joking directly for the body. Slapstick – comic violence or extravagantly physical humour – is named after the Renaissance prop paddle built to sound a sharp crack upon contact with its hapless victim. In *One Man, Two Guvnors*, the role of Alfie, an ancient waiter, allows for a string of physical comedy moments in the dining scene. One includes a sequence in which the speed on Alfie's pacemaker has been dialled up, causing him to dodder aimlessly in sped-up motion around the stage, ultimately coming into inadvertent contact with a swinging cricket bat (and this segment is included in the linked Show Clips). This is literally a modern-day slapstick, in performance producing a sonic crack, which, along with the actor's (Tom Edden in the first cast and video) reaction is likely to draw a gasp from the audience along with a huge laugh. The sharpness of the blow, its adept staging, and the actor's carrying through of response embody a theatricalised image of sudden random violence to an elderly restaurant employee, without perceived risk of real-life pain and suffering.

Such safely delivered brutality has long been the understanding by which audiences accept conventional joking intent. Another participant in the *One Man, Two Guvnors* stage world provides an interesting variation on the delivery and reception of comic violence. During the dinner scene, Francis enlists an apparent audience member, named Christine Patterson, to help with his stage business. By the end of the snowballing, end-of-act excitement, she has been set on fire, doused with water, had her head plunged into a plate of jelly and been covered by the contents of a fire extinguisher. Although we might expect conscripted audience members to endure some degree of embarrassment in the name of crowd amusement, most spectators would draw the line well before the indignities described above. Whether or not any given spectator knows in advance or realises along the way that Christine is an audience plant (she takes a curtain call), the actor's ability to adopt a convincing non-performative demeanour emphasises the very principles of slapstick violence – we trust that no one really gets hurt and that even the victims are in on the joke.

It is clear that the parameters regarding violence-for-amusement have been redrawn over the past half century. In *Breaking Bad* there is straight-ahead slapstick: obsessed by the presence of a fly in his state-of-the-art, underground meth lab, Walt lunges at it from the catwalk, missing, then body-slamming off one of the tanks and onto his back. The initial, flailing tumble, an ultra-clean, one-two crash through to his neat if jarring arrival on the ground and lack of notable injury, all in the context of his driven pursuit of the insect throughout the episode, make for a sudden puncturing of tension via plainly comic intrusion.

At the same time, there is something gruesomely farcical about the double act of Walt and Jesse attempting to dispose of a drug thug's dead body without leaving any traces. In brutal contrast to our species-proud aspirations, physical comedy in the post-Tarantino era exposes the human body in all its gross inelegance: a sack of hard and soft parts, always heavier and messier than you'd think. A film like *Kick-Ass* (2010) treats us with tongue in cheek to the blood-bursting spectacle of an unfortunate thug condemned to death by microwave. Even for contexts like *Jackass* (2000–), in which the injuries are real and sometimes serious enough, the pranksters themselves supply their own ring of laughter around each new ill-advised stunt.

For the YouTube generation, however, laughter can be seen to take a few more steps towards the truly heartless. Many a shared online clip offers bizarrely unfortunate physical mishaps for the amusement of online spectators, with no disclaimer that neither humans nor animals have gone unharmed in the process, and not necessarily any waivers on record for their 15 minutes of humiliation. Comment streams under the videos often include discussions (which is to say, arguments) about the nature of funniness and its opposite, never, of course, to be resolved one way or the other.

The clown figure

There is another aspect of *One Man, Two Guvnors* worth discussing in the context of popular comic performance. Like the once-proud *commedia* practice that Goldoni either buried or saved by fully scripting performance, the play is littered with opportunities for comic virtuosity, especially by the 'One Man' of the title, filled in the original production by actor, writer and television presenter James Corden. Although the role would allow for any such comically gifted character to thrive, Corden's extra-theatrical status is worth emphasising in a discussion of theatre and laughter. It highlights the radical extent to which the specific conditions, histories and even chemistries of the participants exert an impact on any given theatre-and-laughter equation.

Robert Provine, who supplied the neuroscientific perspective earlier, submits that 'laughter has more to do with relationships than with jokes' (Provine, 2000, 3). Although taken from a context of interpersonal transaction, this contention seems applicable in a salient way for an audience going to see a comedy in which the starring role is taken by someone of renown, whom you might already think is funny, and who is right there in the room with you. Based on an Italian prototype, Francis as role-plus-actor derives from the lineage of his English cousin, the Shakespearean clown. Corden did not so much 'lose himself' in the character as subsume the fictional guise into his own popular persona, very much a modern-day relative of, say, Will Kemp as Falstaff.

Most clowns, whatever else they do, experiment at the fulcrum that balances self-deprecation and joking at the audience's expense. The former tends to earn the clown more leverage with regard to the latter, and so joking at the expense of the spectator(s) comes largely on the premise that the clown as comic host picks up the tab for the occasional laugh. As presenter for *A League of Their Own* (2010–) a male-dominated comedy-driven television sports quiz show, Corden has proven a deft improviser, with the wit to supply a topping riposte as well as an awareness as to the occasional value of accepting ridicule upon oneself.

Francis was described prior to his first entrance in *One Man, Two Guvnors* as overweight, and Corden has never made any apology for his inclination towards chubbiness. With *zanni* characters traditionally motivated by hunger, it proves a neat variation on the original model to cast someone whose constant appetite appears to refer to a love of eating, rather than a state of perpetual privation. At one point, Bean's text updates a short scene from Goldoni's original, in which Truffaldino shyly attempts to woo his female counterpart, Smeraldina, named Dolly in the adaptation. Francis sidles up to Dolly (Susie Toaze), and paints a verbal picture of a lovelorn young man who is having trouble mustering the nerve to let his feelings be known (once again, see 'Show Clips'). Dolly, of course, is well aware that it is Francis he is describing, and she is receptive to the advances. In this production, Dolly/Toaze casually touched up her makeup, asking, 'Does he prefer eating or making love?' (65), pausing after 'or' and turning to him for the last two words to unleash the full force of her pulchritude. Corden's fixed-gaze silence was always likely to bring a good-sized audience laugh as his lips seemed to be trying to form some kind of response to a question that would seem to have but one possible answer. Finally, he turned to the audience for, 'It's a tough one, that, isn't it?' The punch line is well written – reversing the general expectation of a leering rejoinder – and its delivery effectively blurred any distinction between actor and character. In this case, the usual reduction of a subject to base, physical desire is itself brought low by the dark-horse consideration of that other possibility we might suspect Francis/Corden to favour. Laughter ultimately remains bound to everyone and everything going on in the room in which it occurs, with no conceivable detail or nuance of context bracketed. It is, however, a completely different story when it appears on the other side of the theatre transaction.

Laughter in the frame

Laughter, as we have seen, is considered the quintessential bodied expression of play or non-seriousness, and has become broadly imported by social interaction as a tool for conscious or semi-conscious communication. It can be taken in conversation to pack as much meaning as the words it accompanies – think, for example, how laughter might affect otherwise serious statements like, 'It's not funny' or 'I'm going to kill you'. From within the theatre frame, then, it can prove quite the potent signifier, throwing up questions about who exactly is doing the laughing, at the same time revelatory of societal and cultural influences.

In the introduction to a collection of essays about literary or theatrical treatments of laughter, Manfred Pfister expresses a belief that,

> the representations of laughter reveal the fault-lines of the anxieties and the social pressures at work at a given historical moment more distinctly than actual laughter does. After all, they do not only 'represent' the laughter of a particular society, but at the same time give a pointed

and pregnant shape to it, analyse and frequently
problematise it. What they also demonstrate is
that actual laughter itself always contains a more
or less marked element of self-conscious performance and theatrical representation, complete
with actors and audiences. (Pfister, 2002, vii)

We can begin with the ways in which playwrights have
written laughter into character and situation, one always
helping to reveal the other. In Tennessee Williams' *The
Glass Menagerie* (1944) Amanda Wingfield uses laughter to
advertise her plantation-bred, feminised effervescence for
the benefit of the Gentleman Caller. Tom 'laughs wildly'
at his mother's prim disapproval of D.H. Lawrence and Jim
'laughs gently' as his interlude with Laura drifts towards
intimacy. In *Six Characters in Search of an Author* (*Sei personaggi
in cerca d'autore*, 1921) Luigi Pirandello employs laughter
to keep the lines fuzzy between life and art. The Step-
Daughter 'bursts out laughing' at the sight of the Leading
Actress attempting to impersonate her in theatrical terms.
The full company laughs at Madame Pace's larger-than-
stage-life presence and speech, adding a further twist to
Pirandello's Möbius-strip rumination upon reality and
artistic artifice.

Beckett, master of laughology, gives us a few more things
worth thinking about here. In *Krapp's Last Tape* (1958) the
title character joins in with several laughs on a recording of
his younger self's birthday thoughts, posing rehearsal que-
ries for director and actor about 'laughing with', 'laughing

at', and (possibly) our encrusted behavioural patterns. Amid Beckett's stage directions in *Happy Days* (1961), we find:

> WINNIE (*Murmur.*) God. (*Pause.* WILLIE *laughs quietly. After a moment she joins in. They laugh quietly together.* WILLIE *stops. She laughs on a moment alone.* WILLIE *joins in. They laugh together. She stops.* WILLIE *laughs on a moment alone. He stops. Pause. Normal voice.*) (150)

An interesting little dialogue transpires between Winnie and Willie, constructed with mathematical symmetry, while demanding transactional excavation in rehearsal. It could easily slide beneath superficial notice, yet leads to Winnie's ensuing admission, 'Ah well what a joy in any case to hear you laugh again, Willie, I was convinced I never would, you never would'. Something important about these two, individually and together, reveals itself pending the actual choices in production. A line later Winnie says, 'How can one better magnify the Almighty than by sniggering with him at his little jokes, particularly the poorer ones?', in one swoop turning the supreme being into every insecure boss who desperately needed our laughter to keep his mask of authority in place.

In recent times, the paper-thin theatre frames of one-on-one theatre offered by companies like Punchdrunk (England) and Anu Productions (Ireland) mean that any laughter between actor and spectator is all but unmediated as far as the body is concerned, sometimes making for revealing iterations of its personal, social and cultural 'meanings'. Anu's *Vardo* (2014) offered the spectator an immersive journey through the underworld of human trafficking and prostitution in modern-day Dublin, a good proportion of which takes place in plain view of real-life passers-by. It was played out on city streets, the bus terminal, a trafficker's car and a small flat on the other side of town. During at least one performance laughter poured from a boozy woman of the streets in the darkness of a pub, hoping to establish grounds for asking a favour; it shot from the mouth of an aggressive sex-trade enforcer as a final warning before physical violence; it forced its way out of an undocumented sex worker in the kitchen of a seamy flat, trying with a little too much effort to entice a mark; it came from real-world bystanders at the bus station, not sure what to make of this strange unfolding scene; and it emerged unbidden from the spectator, finding himself caught between frames of fictional intrigue and bodied discomfort. Laughter was enjoined in all its dialogic, self-revealing immediacy for each of the hundreds of one-on-one performances that transpired during a three-week run.

Laughter as behavioural meme

The sound of laughter has inspired its share of playful experimentation by composers and musicians, often themselves amusing defamiliarisations with something to say about the bodied original. Provine lists 57 'Operas and vocal works with laughter in score, libretto or performance' (Provine, 2001, 73–4), including Leonard Bernstein's *Candide*,

Johann Strauss's *Der Fledermaus* and Wolfgang Amadeus Mozart's *Cosi Fan Tutte*. Laughter often shows off the voice as expressive instrument, capable of high swoops and virtuosic runs, and so we find musical compositions in which laughter is voiced by musical instrumentation; we all know the descending series of unmuted trumpet notes (wah-wah-wah-wah) that underscores abject misfortune for a Looney Tunes character.

As far as the body goes, the robots in Karel Čapek's *R.U.R.* (1921) do not laugh, a defining element of their faux-humanity. Sophie Treadwell's *Machinal* (1928) offers an expressionistic vision of a Young Woman and her systemic suffocation by an unthinking, unfeeling society, anaesthetised by routine and programmed by capitalist, patriarchal ideology. The text includes built-in opportunities to outline the encrusted patterns of mechanised response. In an office situation the four workers supply several group laughs, one prompted by the boss, Mr Jones: 'I'm never in a hurry – That's how I get ahead! (*Laughs. They all laugh.*)' (Treadwell, 4) Mr Jones marries the Young Woman and his laugh takes on creepier undertones in the honeymoon suite: 'Well – you don't want people looking in, do you? (*Laughs.*)' (22). In potential contrast, the Young Woman laughs only in Scene Seven, in intimate circumstances with her lover. With technology firmly in our heads by the 1980s, Max Headroom, the computer-generated TV host, made laughter unsettling *and* laughable, using computer glitches to emphasise and distort the already repetitive nature of the human response.

It is worth at least a nod in the direction of everyday performance in our techno-centric culture, with regard to which it is impossible to ignore the analytical potential for laughter in social media. We have, on the one hand, fallen prey to the irresistible pull of a joking setup (I have seen a late-night Facebook comment stream turn into a brutal 25-pun pileup). On the other, we perform laughter every time we text, 'Ha-ha', or type it into a comment box. This is laughter expressed orthographically, a now conventional transcript of the bodied splash of which partners in virtual dialogue are deprived. There is no doubt a non-Duchenne aspect to it, in that something in our communicative impulse has demanded an utterance be placed on record. It can, of course, be derisive, as well, to signal that the correspondent has missed the point or otherwise lost face; it can be a demonstration of deference; and sometimes, alas, it means, 'I suspect what I just wrote is not that funny ...'. We seem, in this day of texting, posting and chatting, unable to do without the communicative back-up of laughter evident in a smiley emoticon or a keyboard acronym like, 'lol'.

Laughter as theme

Laughter has been deployed for broader thematic resonance in ways that pertain to Freud's enshrinement of humour as our psychic shield against the slings and arrows of adversity: 'Humour is not resigned; it is rebellious. It signifies not only the triumph of the ego but also of the pleasure principle, which is able here to assert itself against the unkindness of the real circumstances' (Freud, 1990, 429). In Freud's take on humour, the super-ego sets aside its customarily stern administrative duties to keep the vulnerable ego afloat through hostile waters. Laughter's swell of pleasure derives from the sudden dispersal of the psychic effort required to manage oncoming suffering.

Tom Murphy's play, *A Thief of a Christmas* (1985), embodies this rebellious spirit in laughter while calling for an extraordinary feat of individual and collective embodied laughing in performance. Set in a once-upon-a-time rural Ireland, the play carries the subtitle, *The Actuality of how Bailegangaire came by its appellation.* Amid the host of regulars at the local public house and gathering place on a stormy night during hard times is Séamus Costello, described as,

> *a fine big man, a bit overweight, in his late thirties. The main feature of his character is his great laugh. (As is frequent in gatherings there is someone with an unusual sounding laugh, an infectious laugh.) COSTELLO's laugh explodes in the air — a great rumble — before going flying up into a cackling falsetto. Indeed, even at a distance, when people see or hear him approaching, an involuntary gurgle of laughter starts in their throats.* (Murphy, 1993b, 179)

Costello becomes the hometown favourite in an epic laughing contest, initiated by a man identified as the Stranger, who, along with his wife, has happened into the pub because of the night's terrible travelling conditions. Clearly the livelier of the two contestants, Costello persists hubristically after he would seem to have won the competition. The final topic, 'misfortune', leads to a harrowing chorus of all the adversity the town and its inhabitants have endured, culminating in:

> Briars to take out your eyes!
> Or to bate the children with!
> Put smacht (*manners*) on them when there's
> nought for their bellies!
> Miadh, misfortunes!
> An' there's more to come! (236)

The stageful of laughing bodies create a communal act of repudiating reality, as Freud puts it, the prising open of a gap in which each new real-life misery hurled onto the runaway train of group mirth sits that much more uneasily with wave upon wave of laughter. Costello's climactic shout, 'Send us your best!' (236), appears to meet with swift and tragic retribution from above, as (Warning: Spoiler Alert) he collapses and dies.

The play's companion piece, *Bailegangaire* (1985), itself subtitled, *The Story of Bailegangaire and how it came by its appellation*, centres around the same event, removed in time and representation, as it is told years later. Mommo, who we discover was the Stranger's Wife all those years ago, is now bedridden and senile. She tells the story in ragged, half-distracted bursts of the night Bailegangaire earned its name, which is Irish, she explains, for 'the place without laughter' (Murphy, 1993a, 92). We discover the night had further cosmic cruelty to mete out, leaving her alone to raise two granddaughters, Mary and Dolly, who have struggled for decades with failed dreams and mutual resentment against the death grip of the past.

Mommo may well have foresworn the company of laughter since that night, only ever producing a bitter facsimile at the beginning of the play: '(*and there is defiance, hatred in the sound*). Heh heh heh heh. (93)', and in the 2014 Druid production, Marie Mullen shot out the syllables like blunt-edged bullets, chin thrust forward. The act of laughing is more present through narration and citation in this play, but the long day's night of frustration and disappointment leads to a new understanding between Mary and Dolly. They consummate their reborn sisterhood in gales of shared, unrestrained laughter, foregrounded directorially by Garry Hines in the Druid production and played by Catherine Walsh (Mary) and Aisling O'Sullivan (Dolly). Here laughter's psychological and socialising dual-action agency is placed on theatrical display, a boisterous, restorative image of its capacity to save us from the terrifying prospect of facing life's serial adversities alone.

Two other contemporary plays worth noting exemplify polarised views of laughter's nature and purpose. Peter Barnes' *Laughter!* (1978) sets out a fully contemptuous take on the title subject, with broadly comic clichés and searing indictment taking turns undercutting one another. From lights-up an 'immaculately dressed Author with notes' attempts to address the audience:

> AUTHOR: Ladies and Gentlemen ...
> *A hand slaps a large custard pie straight in his face. As he wipes it off a laughing Voice declares: It's going to be that kind of a show, folks!*
> No it isn't. Gangrene has set in. Comedy itself is the enemy. Laughter only confuses and corrupts everything we try to say. It cures nothing except our consciences and so ends by making the nightmare worse. A sense of humour's no remedy for evil. Isn't that why the Devil's always smiling? (Barnes, 1989, 343)

Harsh and fatalistic, this play imagines episodes from the brutal historical chapters of Ivan the Terrible and Adolph Hitler, with laughter offering little more than a fleeting hollow triumph for the doomed. Barnes would appear to have no patience for the Freudian position: 'Laughter's too feeble a weapon against the barbarities of life. A balm for battles lost, standard equipment for the losing side; the powerful have no need of it' (343).

Sarah Ruhl conversely awards laughter a romantic, chimerical status, in which even its killing force is somehow life-affirming. *The Clean House* (2007) takes place in a 'metaphysical Connecticut', where Matilde, a young Brazilian housekeeper, is infinitely more interested in devising the perfect joke than cleaning. Matilde recalls the distinctive bond of love between her parents:

> My mother and father did not look into each other's eyes. They laughed like hyenas. Even when they made love they laughed like hyenas. My mother was old for a mother. She refused many proposals. It would kill her, she said, to have to spend her days laughing at jokes that were not funny. (Ruhl, 9)

As Matilde knows her mother died laughing at one of her father's jokes, she ultimately puts her own perfect joke to merciful use. Laughter in all its soul-baring physical excess is the answer both to life *and* death in Ruhl's world.

These few pointed cases merely skim the surface of laughter's potential as embodied opening upon our many shades of humanity. For now, we'll look at one recent entry to help with the transition from laughter to the concept of funniness. Owen McCafferty's *Death of a Comedian* (2015) presents an up-and-coming stand-up comic, whose girlfriend acts as his manager, supplying aesthetic guidance and reality checks. The pull of stardom inevitably leads him into the clutches of an agent, depicted as a Mephistophelian echo of soul-poaching temptation. The play drives a wedge between a pure spirit of funniness as embodiment of a roughly hewn individual comic vision, and the irresistible dream of commercial stand-up success, which by definition means the sacrifice of any authentic personal spark.

The play begins with the Comedian practising an element of his routine, before succumbing to an attack of self-doubt:

> COMEDIAN … what if i'm not funny
> GIRLFRIEND you are funny
> COMEDIAN what does that mean
> GIRLFRIEND you're a funny person
> COMEDIAN a funny person – i don't want
> to be a funny person i want to be a comedian.
> (McCafferty, 13)

The Comedian, in his will to perfection, fails to realise the true meaning inherent in the distinction between funny person and professional comedian. This does, of course, describe the wavering tightrope to be walked by any would-be mainstream comic. Laughter for a widest possible audience in a commercial, global context almost certainly requires concessions to commodification. The Agent says to the couple in no uncertain terms, 'i need both of you – to know – and i mean to really know – that i know what i'm talking about that i know comedy – i know this fucking business'. (31) Again, the distinction muscles the definition of comedy – the bankable production of laughter with a sufficiently lucrative market share – towards some homogenised notion of laughter provocation, and away from a purer, playful personal take on the ways of the world. Here the laughter to which the Girlfriend aspires is positioned closer to some 'true' concept of funniness than the laughter

sold to stadium audiences by the Agent – and so the metaphoric death foreshadowed in the play's title comes at the
moment of greatest outward success.

Funniness

And so on to the problematic concept of funniness. We usually know when someone has *tried* to make a joke, through
facial, vocal or linguistic cues (and sometimes someone will
try to claim joking intent after the fact, having been genuinely misapprehended or caught crossing a line). Make no
mistake, though: a joke in and of itself has no inherent or
transcending coefficient of funniness, and is therefore in no
possible scenario a scientific measurement for 'a sense of
humour'. John Limon has formulated a set of forthright and
fitting criteria for an analysis of, as it happens, stand-up comedy. They help cut to the core of potential arguments about
what we can presume as essentially 'funny' – the answer
being, nothing. Limon theorises: 'If you think something is
funny, it is' (Limon, 11).

Limon maintains a focus on stand-up performance, and
so I would like to enlist his tools for the more expansive
issue of funniness in theatre and everywhere else. The idea
of something being deemed funny because it has garnered
some critical mass of laughter from an audience can be useful to some extent, but remains endlessly beholden to the
details of context. A racist joke made at a Ku Klux Klan rally
is likely to score high in the laughter department, thereby
qualifying as 'successful' humour *in that context*. The joke
and its response recounted later that week on *Last Week*

Tonight with John Oliver (2014–) will no doubt fare poorly with the studio audience, as the former in-group comes to occupy the minority position; it is somehow likely to be flipped by Oliver to turn ridicule upon the original jokers and laughers. But any given television viewer at home may laugh, not laugh, laugh and feel bad about it, laugh politely (depending on whom she is watching it with), and so on. 'Funny', quite simply, is not an actual property of things, people, places or ideas.

Limon's first theorem, 'If you think something is funny, it is', presumes alternatively that if you think something is *not* funny, it is not. This and Limon's second theorem, 'A joke is funny if and only if you laugh at it' (12) appropriately direct our attention away from abstract generalising and towards the hereness of the occurrence. The point is that there is little about laughter that can be taken for granted outside its particular circumstances.

We can certainly know that something was intended to be funny, but, as suggested above, everyone party to a humorous transaction may express a different position on its funniness, possibly through laughter – and sometimes through, as Michael Billig has called it, 'unlaughter': '"Unlaughter" can be used to describe a display of not laughing when laughter might otherwise be expected, hoped for or demanded' (Billig, 192). Laughter always bears rhetorical meaning, although sometimes not as the laugher intends, and Billig emphasises that, 'we are the laughing animal only because we are also the unlaughing one' (7). Unlaughter constitutes a bodied response to a humour attempt, and it differs from the non-response to a joke we don't get or have heard before or think just isn't very good. It is an upsurge of some opposite of amusement, usually at a subject we feel is tasteless, inappropriate or insulting. (For the record, 'Can't you take a joke?' is one of the more shameless catch phrases of social bullying.)

Having exported Limon's criteria with minor de-customising for a broader context, I shall add one of my own: nothing funny can be fully separated from its performance context (and Limon did not need this one, because his area of focus was specifically the stand-up contract). This claim, for the purpose of efficiency and impact, may expand the notion of performance to include whatever purposeful framing has gone into its arrangement on the page, its editing on film and video or its fashioning on the stage.

Laughter and context

So context is everything to a radical extent, not only to the laughter itself in response to a joking utterance, but to the notion of ethics in play with regard to who makes the joke, who laughs, at whose expense, within what social situation and what cultural framing, among other details.

At the start of *Women and Laughter*, Frances Gray leads us down a feminist-friendly garden path in her telling of Baubo's bold success at making the inconsolable Demeter laugh, as related in the ancient Eleusinian Mysteries. In Gray's version Baubo is a cheeky serving maid who has staged a show for the grieving goddess, 'telling smutty jokes, parodying the pains of pregnancy and birth, and finally producing from beneath her skirts Demeter's little son' (Gray, 1), which, in causing her laughter, led to the cyclical earthly renewal of Spring.

'Thus comedy was born', Gray seems to conclude, proceeding to connect it to a distinctly female laughter:

> A story of a lost matriarchal paradise, you might say, a rich female culture in which one woman heals another, and ultimately Nature itself, by inventing comedy, a comedy joyously and benevolently sexual without being sexist. (1–2)

Gray then bursts her own rhetorical bubble by pulling back focus to paint a broader contextual picture of an insistently patriarchal culture, in which women are a 'tolerated minority', far less than central to the rites within which the stories are told:

> Laughing female sexuality is male-defined as something to be transcended, a last reminder of the base body before the spirit moves on to higher things. In this scenario the role of Baubo is played by a woman not because it celebrates female strength but because it is beneath male dignity. (2)

Gray's take on the myth reminds us not to become dazzled by the close-up, to look for those sometimes hidden lines of power in the joking configuration. How does in-group and out-group status map to the participants at each layer of the contextual onion?

The US television series, *It's Always Sunny in Philadelphia* (2005–), bases each episode's comic arc upon central characters who stake out through word and action some project which represents a direct challenge to an aspect or issue of contemporary society (always prefigured with exceeding bluntness in the title as, for example, 'The Gang Finds a Dead Guy', 'The Gang Finds a Dumpster Baby', or 'Charlie's Mom Has Cancer'). The episode usually unwinds into a fantasia of absurd consequence, often involving unhealthy doses of inebriation, carnal indulgence and moral repugnance. The Gang consists of a brother and sister and two friends as four twenty-something reluctant owners and operators of Paddy's Irish Pub in the title city; the siblings' father (played by Danny DeVito) is the appetite-driven, amoral con man, who almost always shows them how a pro would do it in the most venal, self-serving manner. The Gang, in a way, form a five-headed trickster figure, duplicitous, hedonistic and pursuing each scheme to fantastic extents. One presumes they are intended to expose with comic excess the worst-case products of materialistic, superficial American culture, driven by ignorance, self-interest and the arrogance of middle-class, white privilege. In the broader fictional context of the show they remain more or less isolated in a world of their own – in most cases the characters they come up against remain either unmoved or downright appalled by their behaviours. This makes for an interesting tension with comic potencies previously sampled in TV shows like *The Office* and *Curb Your Enthusiasm*. From a laughter perspective, the vital question is, who is watching at any given television set or computer screen – and, importantly, can they perceive an ironic distance between the characters' utterances and a broader moral compass from which we are meant to access amusement?

It is always worth asking, especially with boldly aired social, moral and ethical issues at stake: to what extent are all parties to the transaction playing the same game, as it were? Richard Pryor did a routine in 1976 called, 'Bicentennial Prayer' (which can be found at the link in the Bibliography). It sounds like a small or modestly sized venue with an audience all or largely African American. Pryor begins by caricaturing the quasi-musical cadence of a Southern Baptist preacher: 'We are … gathered here today … to celebrate this year of our centenniality … in the hope of freedom and dignity. We are celebrating two hundred years …'. At this point he slides into something more like his own voice to complete the sentence, 'of white folks kickin' ass'. Pryor returns to the preaching mode and soon arrives at, 'we offer this prayer, and the prayer is: How long will this bullshit go on?' Pryor's audience sounds pre-emptively entertained by the send-up of churchified oration, but the no-nonsense punch lines receive peak laughter responses. The fervent sense of petition with regard to God's mysterious ways is effectively laid bare by the plain truth of the matter, and plays well to Pryor's loyal audience – especially those who can identify first hand with the unmasking of certain American citizens' positions in a society largely thrilled with itself on the two-hundredth anniversary of its founding upon principles that, for them, remained quite a bit short of fully realised.

About 35 years later, stand-up comic Louis C.K. begins one of his routines by acknowledging to the audience that he has a lot going for him: 'I'm healthy, I'm relatively young, I'm white … which, thank God for that shit, boy.' C.K. goes on to expand upon how much he loves being white (see link in Bibliography): 'Seriously, if you're not white, you're missing out because this shit is thoroughly good. Let me be clear, by the way. I'm not saying that white people are better. I'm saying that being white is *clearly* better – who could even argue? If it was an option, I'd re-up every year, "Oh, yeah, I'll take white again, absolutely. Enjoying that, I'm gonna stick with white, thank you"'.

One critical view holds that we should only call an utterance properly ironic if there is someone, real or imagined, who stands to take it solely at face value, rather than *also* as its sly opposite. C.K.'s audience was probably largely white and could conceivably buy in directly to a self-serving relief at being declared lucky winners of the racial-prerogative sweepstakes. It is likely, though, that his fans would perceive the impolitic bluntness of the observation (captured in the alternative-reality framing that skin colour is one of today's abundance of choices, so by all means, choose wisely), and that some part of the laughter would acknowledge the shameful social reality of persistent white privilege from which they benefit. Both routines use 'truth-telling' strategies, and both these audiences, though different in the laughter valences for obvious reasons, essentially comprise in-group crowds.

Clever framings may drill home points in comically astute ways, with a comedian's likely audience quite willing to endorse the sentiment. The mainstream theatre provides an altogether different model of demographic probability as far as audiences go, with important ramifications for comic licence. Whatever else has been thought of his work, Martin McDonagh's stage output over the past two decades has proven a scholar's blessing for studies of taste, offence and laughter. Having grown up in London to Irish parents, who would bring him to summer in Connemara in the west of Ireland, McDonagh's work can always be counted upon to stimulate discussion of, 'Who is allowed to joke?'

McDonagh's 2010 play, *A Behanding in Spokane*, is set in a country (the United States) in which he was neither raised nor connected through parents and summer holidays. The play contains McDonagh's customary mix of characters' unvarnished self-interest and deception, petty quibbling amid violent threat, and, in particular, offensive repartee of various ilks from the mouths of unenlightened characters. Here he places a young couple in a hotel room way out of their depth as far as low-level scamming goes, in that it is occupied by a psychotic white supremacist who has for quite a long time been looking for his severed left hand. The young man of the couple, who is African American, has come to claim the reward – even though the missing appendage he has brought along appears an unlikely match in coming from a black person. There can be no question of comic intent in McDonagh's script – it is what the writer does, and other reviews attest to it. One spectator, however, a reviewer from the *New Yorker* magazine, expressed undisguised contempt for what he perceived as a degrading representation of the young black man and for the 'vile' proliferation of 'n'-words in the name of comedy. The critic zeroes in on the principle of othering inherent in comic characterisation, with its dicey implications for today's pluralistic societies:

> McDonagh adds gag after gag to the show, as if he believed that comedy could cover up the real horror at its core: the fact that blackness is, for him, a Broadway prop, an easy way of establishing a hierarchy. Like any smart immigrant, McDonagh knows that by going after Toby's otherness he becomes less of an outsider himself. (Als)

The review by *New Yorker* critic, Hilton Als, is what unlaughter looks like in print. At the very least it shows that joking licence is awarded on a strictly subjective basis, but it airs some issues well worth thinking about with regard to joking rights, social demographics and the ethics of comic representation.

The above issue is no passing quibble, but lies at the heart of why acts of apparent frivolity are worth picking apart. As Hurley, Dennett and Adams point out, we use laughter-based strategies as ways of checking what we consider key personality features, knowledge, preferences, dispositions and opinions in new acquaintances and potential partners: 'Humor is a particularly efficient and reliable – though not foolproof – quick probe. The role of humor as a relatively hard-to-fake or costly signal in mate assessment is thus not hard to discern' (268). Through our joking and laughter we ascertain who thinks and feels like us, often through the targeting of those who do not. It is all the more imperative to think about why we laugh, *if* we laugh in theatre and performance situations, because of the exponentially broader impact about what thought lines and prejudices we cannot seem to help but endorse. And, as shown in this section, it is especially worthwhile to consider what or whom a production thinks it *can* joke about, expecting the ratification of mass audience laughter.

Laughter as crowd control

The preceding point notwithstanding, the social pleasures of subjects bonding in playful contexts would seem one of the more ingenuous aspects of laughter in the theatre. There remains, however, the fact that laughter at even the most rebellious comic utterances ends at some point, seeing those involved returned safely to society's normal service. Billig makes a direct connection to the master projects of late capitalist culture and the nurturing of a sort of feel-good sense of rebellion mined insidiously by commercially produced laughter:

> The more we laugh and the more we imagine ourselves to be daringly free in the moments of our laughter, the more we are complying with the demands of the so-called free market. And the more we reveal ourselves captive to the demand that we possess a naughty sense of humour. (212)

Whether the laughter of an audience is seen to reify or challenge the scripts of the status quo, the effect appears the same: the subject is lost to any orderly sense of social bearing, a potential wild card of thought and feeling, which simultaneously renders it unable to mobilise and therefore entirely vulnerable. When the laughter's charge is triggered by ridicule or the like, a double-bind effect seems to be in operation: in accepting an invitation to an in-group's pleasure club we surrender to a state of bodied submission.

Billig suggests that we inscribe our children with rules and ideologies through regimes of embarrassment (i.e., being laughed at), so that they can then take their rightful places in a society that polices itself by mocking difference (i.e., laughing at others). Who sponsors laughter, who allows and commissions it, cannot be separated from its power relations. Indira Ghose writes insightfully on Shakespeare and laughter, and one of her contentions, that, 'The main function of laughter in the Shakespearean theatre was to create social cohesion within an audience drawn from all ranks of society' (4), may be relevant to a discussion of laughter and panto performance, one of the more populist theatrical forms. The Christmas panto, a seasonal theatre tradition in the UK and Ireland, promises music, laughter and, in prime venues, a star or two of TV fame. Designed to appeal to an audience of all ages, it toys with the moveable parts of a fairy-tale narrative and, comedy-wise, ventures both cheeky, topical barbs and more mainstream joking about, say, dwarves, wicked stepsisters or whatever ready-made targets the story brings along. With a brief of 'pure entertainment', the yearly panto can be seen both as populist vehicle for communal celebration and rite of re-enlistment in the approved social order.

Ghose makes a vital point about the linking of play and laughter in pleasure and the usual assumption that laughter is opposed to seriousness:

> I suggest that one of the most insidious fallacies is the belief that laughter is trivial. The function of laughter is to *make* things trivial – and thus gain mastery over whatever threatens to overwhelm us. (Ghose, 2008, 7)

Ghose is talking here about laughter's potential to manage psychic threat, but there is reason to consider this suggestion from a more cynical, social perspective. The re-framing that brings about laughter can be applied externally for a sort of controlled, carnival effect, which limits the social space a threatening idea is given while branding it as non-serious.

Michel Foucault's concept of biopolitical 'technologies' suggests strategies of power-wielding which have sought to control the population by means other than direct physical threat – through, for example, the inscription in the populace of sexual 'norms'. Recall Bergson's distillation of humorous laughter's herding instinct on behalf of social propriety: 'Laughter is above all a corrective. Being intended to humiliate, it must make a painful impression on the person against whom it is directed' (187). Laughter, seen in this way, might be one of the shrewdest technologies of power ever harnessed: through laughter we make sure that no one strays too far from approved thought and comportment, literally giving over our bodies to the laughter that keeps *others* in line and the threat of being laughed at that keeps *us* in line.

Laughter as event

In the search for a countervailing hope to the dispiriting views of theatre and laughter just aired, we can latch onto one of Sutton-Smith's concluding remarks, that 'play is typically a primary place for the expression of anything that is humanly imaginable' (226). Within a theatre context, this concept finds expression in the words of phenomenologist Bruce Wilshire, who contends that, 'We beings – we actual beings – discover our power over possibility. Together the audience and the actors engage in incarnated imaginative variation on the meaning of human being and doing' (24). On the laughter side, anthropologist Mary Douglas claims, 'a joke implies that anything is possible' (373). By suspending real-world limits through the agency of play, theatre and laughter retain the capacity to blow open the doors of possibility – and it is a contention of this argument that once the horse is out of the barn, you can never quite squeeze all of it back inside.

A practical guide to comic politics is hard to come by – one can find theorists who will point out that a joke's ridicule can be aimed 'downward' from majority or 'upward'

from minority in-groups, thereby representing conserva-
tive and subversive agencies respectively. It is left, then,
to the fictional Eddie Waters, met earlier with reference
to *Comedians*, to offer guidance. World weary, though not
yet having given up the good fight, Eddie demonstrates the
ugliness behind a joke that courts laughter by fatuously rein-
forcing a cheap stereotype about women. Indeed, women,
along with the elderly, the disabled, 'foreigners' (those
visiting and those who live in our midst) and other go-to
joking butts have roused laughter in our theatres from time
immemorial.

Waters then goes on to say, 'a true joke, a comedian's
joke, has to do more than release tension, it has to *liberate*
the will and the desire, it has to *change the situation*' (20). The
advice is clear enough: if your joke simply seeks laughter
through clichéd allusion to the low-hanging fruit of cultural
prejudice, good luck to you; a 'good' joke takes Douglas
at her word to insinuate new spaces into our collective
world view.

Hold onto that thought for a few paragraphs, as we consider Slavoj Žižek's take on the concept of 'event'. While
he is obviously interested in the grand sweep and deeper
thought of sociocultural sea changes, the currents of conventional thought, and their turning points, his argument
cannot help but pique the interest of someone interested in
laughter, humour and what they can or cannot do in the
overall scheme of things. Žižek appears to characterise
the subject in terms at least superficially akin to the way
in which we have seen humour built, in that, 'at its most

elementary, event is not something that occurs within the world, but is *a change of the very frame through which we perceive the world and engage in it*' (10).

Simon Critchley also takes inspiration from Eddie Waters' formulation in support of a two-step claim that drives his ruminations in *On Humour* (2002). He points out, first of all, the pockets of unspoken knowledge and feeling to which humorous laughter gives bodied expression: 'the tiny explosions of humour that we call jokes return us to a common, familiar world of shared practices, the background meanings implicit in a culture' (Critchley, 2002, 16). Critchley, however, goes on to advocate a second feature, evocative of Waters' urging to 'change the situation'. He suggests humour may also 'indicate how those practices might be transformed or perfected, how things might be otherwise. Humour both reveals the situation, and indicates how that situation might be changed' (16). The student of theatre may find an echo in these characterisations of Bertolt Brecht's 'demonstrator', problematising the socially ingrained presumptions of causality in a traffic accident: 'Our demonstrator may at any time be in a position to say: "The driver was guilty, because it all happened the way I showed you. He wouldn't be guilty if it had happened the way I'm going to show you now"' (Brecht, 127).

It is in these terms arguable that a Duchenne laugh at a truly good joke embodies a psychic upheaval that leaves in its wake the slightest reconfiguration of our world view. When Sarah Silverman says to her audience, 'I want to get an abortion. But my boyfriend and I are having trouble conceiving', she is doing more than making a joke about foolishness and a hot-button topic. On the surface, the joke seems to be a dim-thinking reversal of priority between seeking an abortion and getting pregnant. The joke can be seen, however, to ridicule a zealous, simplistic stance on abortion that would have us believe it is something women just like to do. We cannot know whether this joke has ever changed anyone's mind on the subject – probably not – but it does offer a canny reframing of what passes for debate on an extremely serious personal and social issue.

In this way, insightful reframings can bring about small but significant alterations in existing thought fields, whether or not they change opinions. Žižek might not intend his conceit to refer to such mundane, repeatable situations, especially because those in Silverman's audience may be likely to share her general views, even if they hadn't thought of them in quite those terms. In a theatre context, though, once-off events and the digital proliferation of subsequent performances both stand to contribute to the conditions for change. Political persuasion and spheres of spectating become subject to unprecedented dynamics in the age of live transmission, smartphone recording and internet viewing on demand. The *National Theatre Live* series allows for productions like the aforementioned *One Man, Two Guvnors* to play special performances, for which audiences geographically removed from London's West End attend a live transmission in a cinema. We can imagine the implications for this outer band of spectators with regard to a study of theatre and laughter: the experience imparts a sense of 'being there' at the performance, but processing is mediated by camera angles, and laughter in the live-transmission audience happens at a remove, deprived of the open channel between stage and auditorium. Parties to the transaction in London are only aware of the outer audience in that they know they are watching; the 'outer' laughter cannot directly affect the performance, nor does it interact with the internal audience response (though it can, of course, be affected by it).

Stand-up comedy also alters the transactional chemistry for monster venues, in which spectators far from the stage receive an important element of their visual input either from tiny bodies at a distance or big bodies on a large screen. If we include the fandom and commodity-exchange elements in a stand-up audience, it becomes evident that the outer band of spectators who watch an act on DVD or YouTube are subject to a vastly reduced (if not absent) social involvement, and may not have the same commitment to the performer or performance as someone who has purchased tickets. Film and video by definition flatten three-dimensional life, in the process tending to squeeze from it some of the chemical reaction upon which stand-up thrives.

Changing the situation

There arises from recent Irish performance a case worth looking at, related to the lived-through transaction of the theatre event and the outer bands of spectating on the internet, but also relevant to issues of laughter and political agency. This was a one-off performance at the Abbey

Theatre in Dublin, and it took place on the night of
1 February 2014, following the evening's performance of James
Plunkett's, *The Risen People* (1958). The production explored
the human costs for workers and families during the 1913
Dublin Lockout, while paying homage to the collectivising
spirit that drove what is perceived as a memorable moment
in Ireland's social and labour histories. For the production,
the Abbey revived the tradition of the Noble Call in connection with the theme of political action, and so a succession of
artists, journalists, intellectuals and activists took the stage
each night following the show. On the night in question, the
opportunity fell to Irish drag artist Panti (Rory O'Neill) to
deliver the last of the production's Noble Calls. Panti, sometimes known as Panti Bliss, had been a prominent feature
of Ireland's alternative performance landscape for almost
twenty years, and on this night she stood in front of the
assembled cast and introduced herself as follows: 'Hello. My
name is Panti and for the benefit of the visually impaired or
the incredibly naïve, I am a drag queen, I am also, I guess,
a performer of sorts, and an accidental and occasional gay
rights activist' (video link Bibliography).

In fact, it would have been unlikely that anyone in the
audience would not have known who she was, following
almost three weeks of high-visibility controversy. During
the course of a live interview on RTÉ television, Ireland's
national broadcaster, O'Neill had named two journalists
and members of a Catholic lobbying group he considered to
be homophobic. Immediate threats of lawsuits led swiftly
to a public apology by RTÉ and a nominal cash settlement

for the offended parties. Social media saw viral outrage at the apparent shutdown of public discussion, and the absence of transparent explanation for RTÉ's exceedingly quick capitulation.

And then Panti surfaced, unannounced, on the stage of the Abbey, finding in the National Theatre the forum for rebuttal she had been denied in the original medium of contention. Her ten-minute performance was filmed (by Conor Horgan, Caroline Campbell, Nicky Gogan and Ailish Bracken), with the camera following her through the stage door, before taking up an opportune position in the house. From a humour and laughter studies perspective the performance allows for some interesting discussion.

Here we can see a practical application of Provine's observation, discussed above with regard to James Corden in *One Man, Two Guvnors*, that laughter is 'more about relationships than jokes'. Panti/O'Neill would have been well aware of the two different audiences – one in the theatre, one on the web – the performance would be addressing, thereby complicating the joking configuration. Theatregoers purchasing tickets to the Abbey Theatre, with its national identity badge and its commercial remit for broadest possible appeal, would not generally expect to find a drag queen on the bill. The audience would have gone to see a play about a well-known hundredth-anniversary event with quasi-nationalist overtones (and who knows what the tourists made of it?). Unsurprisingly, the video went straight to the top of the virtual charts, transforming an issue that had gained international legs on blogs and social media into a performance deemed worthy of coverage by major media outlets all over the world.

Panti's performance serves as a notable object of study, because of the 'original' audience, for which she could not have predicted the precise demographic makeup, but which was likely to include patrons who had not previously attended a live drag performance and/or may not have been sympathetic to Panti's stand on mainstream homophobia. There are no knock-'em-dead laughs in this performance text and there do not seem to be any raucous responses in the recording – it may not even qualify as a comic text, as the humour is far from ever-present. For the record, no crowd hostility is audibly evident, and the slice of audience caught on camera during the final applause shows some people standing and others simply applauding. While unable to absent myself from a subjective perspective upon video viewing, I have analysed with admiration moments that elicited some degree of audience laughter in what I take to be an astute deployment of humorous utterance.

While Panti's joking style elsewhere has occasion to include rude single entendres, her tone here is disarmingly heartfelt. Her opening words, 'Hello. My name is Panti and for the benefit of the visually impaired or the incredibly naïve, I am a drag queen …' calls pre-emptive, self-deprecating attention to her appearance. A subsequent revelation about her background, 'And although this may surprise some of you, I have always managed to find gainful employment in my chosen field – gender discombobulation', brings a large audience laugh, this time through invocation of a common script from the general area of public speaking, ambushed by a word that is impossible to take seriously, yet lends a useful metaphoric descriptor to the language of queer studies.

Panti's humour is crafted for the mainstream audience she was likely to meet, melting the ice without bringing down the house. With sureness of purpose and lightness of touch she recasts experience to catch the glare of everyday indignities strewn in the wake of heteronormative business as usual: 'Have you ever been on a crowded train with your gay friend and a small part of you is cringing because he is being SO gay and you find yourself trying to compensate by butching up or nudging the conversation onto "straighter" territory?' Emerging with complete seriousness from the mouth of a drag queen, this narrative nugget sets off a comic wobble between homophobic gaze and gay subjectivity, alluding to a cruel culturally enforced self-loathing.

Panti completes the circuit of comic damnation by coming round to the perverse logic inherent in pronouncements by 'straight people – ministers, senators, lawyers, journalists' and their condemnation of her use of the word 'homophobia': 'And a jumped-up queer like me should know that the word "homophobia" is no longer available to gay people. Which is a spectacular and neat Orwellian trick because now it turns out that gay people are not the victims of homophobia – homophobes are'. The surpassing patience of the 'jumped-up queer' turns the phrase's garish cast back upon her attackers as prelude to her equally adept unravelling of their absurdist logic.

The speech's dénouement is quite shrewd, and is worth quoting (almost) in its entirety:

> I do, it is true, believe that almost all of you are probably homophobes. But I'm a homophobe. It would be incredible if we weren't. To grow up in a society that is overwhelmingly homophobic and to escape unscathed would be miraculous. So I don't hate you because you are homophobic. I actually admire you. I admire you because most of you are only a bit homophobic. Which all things considered is pretty good going.

Here we have one final peeling of the onion, the unblinking accusation delivered in performance without any touch of malice; the social comment (which is not so funny); and the eventual reversal into a sort of damning admiration, topped off with an informal flourish that leaves the critique hanging somewhere between deference and bitter irony.

Panti manages to pitch her performance as thoughtful, heartfelt and self-effacing, without giving an inch on politics and principle. The final laugh comes after the most hard-hitting statement, which refers to the speech's ongoing theme of having to 'check' oneself at pedestrian crossings because of lads in passing cars throwing things at her and calling her, 'Fag!' She clearly is not joking when she says it, and feeling rises in her visibly as the performance reaches its payoff: 'I hate myself because I fucking check myself while standing at pedestrian crossings. And sometimes I hate you for doing that to me.' The near-immediate concession, 'But not right now', no doubt refers to the relatively amiable discussion she has been having with the audience; it trades on a sudden downshift of feeling and a relief effect the spectators may well be eager to indulge through laughter.

The performance never meets with (nor aims for) knock-'em-dead laughs. Here, a knack for the subtler arts of humour helps to 'change the situation' through an attempt to disarm, a deft defamiliarization of viewpoint (of which Brecht should have been proud), and a controlled yet strongly felt accusation at the finish, undercut with an equally felt sense of genuine communal playing.

In an account of the event, Fintan Walsh calls attention first to the born-again power of a live theatre event and to the radical reconfiguration of spectating dynamics in the leap to cyberspace: 'While queer performance typically takes place in very localized community contexts, this occasion was striking too insofar as social media and video sharing technologies were instrumental in effectively extending the stage by circulating the performance worldwide, newly expanding lines of influence and impact'. (Walsh, 106) It is likely that people from all corners of the social spectrum watched the performance online, and came to include legions of viewers who would know from personal experience what Panti was talking about. It would be misguided to generalise about audience response to Panti's humour strategies from this sprawling outer band of spectators, and there were no doubt hate responses and comments from those who would be hurling epithets and milk cartons at someone like her waiting to cross the road. Suffice to say that this new and expansive layer of audience has brought with it implications that are difficult to throw an analytical net around but impossible to ignore, because, laugh or not, one cannot unsee or unhear what has been seen and heard.

Discussions about the political potency of humorous laughter often fixate on a big-picture, 'measurable results' kind of scenario in which some sociocultural transformation can be seen to come about as a direct result of a joke, routine or dramatic text. A sudden change in legislation or popular opinion would provide impressive evidence, but is it the only view that means anything? Morreall points to the parallel births of democracy and comedy in fifth-century Athens, and the proliferation of printed satires in the lead-up to the American Revolution. And what *about* something like Sarah Palin's comic decimation by Tina Fey on *Saturday Night Live* (several episodes in 2008 and after), after which Palin's political star began a clear descent? When thought and feeling and body are fully bound up in one of these modest events, it is hard to believe that laughter bounces ineffectually off all participants, dissipates without a trace, and that the person/parties/situation remain precisely the same as if the laughter never happened.

Žižek's notion of Event would offer hope to the Laughter for Change camp, because it has to do with an alteration in our conception of the Real, rather than a change in reality itself. A comedian's joke 'undoes the past itself' (150), in Žižek's words, redraws our perception of the way we got here, in the process adding to the map of potential, so that, 'the truly new emerges through narrative, the apparently purely reproductive retelling of what happened – it is this retelling that opens up the space (the possibility) of acting in a new way' (150). Panti and others will continue to 'check' themselves at pedestrian crossings, but according to this view, the world is drawn differently for those who attended the Abbey performance that night, along with the hundreds of thousands of others who viewed the video evidence. Importantly, even the 'unlaughter' of homophobic trolls suggests that bodies have been breached, leaving thought boundaries reforged ever after.

The preceding analysis hardly constitutes a proof of laughter and theatre's united capacity to alter the course of human thought and feeling, and there are those who would argue strenuously against such a proposition. Again, though, would a forensic connection between a comic utterance and a revolution constitute the only valid evidence for a sense that laughter retains the capacity to serve the underdog or the unfranchised?

Ghose observes that, 'The main affinities between laughter and play lie in the momentary creation of a separate world' (7), and theatre (plus all its performative offshoots) must surely merit inclusion in such an alliance. There are communal and psychic benefits within those concentric magic circles of play, even if they take place amongst the oppressed, powerless, and, in the cases of cabaret performers sent to Nazi prison camps, doomed. Morreall cites recollections from Holocaust survivors regarding such comic performances, which attest to their value in strengthening psychic and social resolve. There are meaningful ways to 'change the situation', without necessarily changing the immediate outcome.

One more thing

Norman Holland, a psychoanalytic critic, tells us that, 'In laughing, we suddenly and playfully recreate our identities' (198). We are what we laugh at, and we are also what we think about laughter. It is, in fact, instances like these that help reveal the degree of problematisation required in discussions of 'funniness'. It does not then matter whether you can totally identify with all my examples and thoughts on them. The only thing one can be sure of is that it is important to think about laughter, to think about society's laughter, and to think about your own laughter, with so much raw data pouring from our mouths every day and everywhere, and with a noteworthy subset of it found in performance situations.

Elsewhere in *The Empty Space*, Peter Brook sets forth an 'acid test' for the power of theatrical image to burn itself into the memory. 'When years later I think of a striking theatrical experience I find a kernel engraved on my memory' (136), he says, going on to recall in thumbnail sketches the lingering images from several recognisable plays. Technological advances since then lead me to report a laughter-specific version of this effect, in the way that I recall memorable comic moments in short, moving clips, which capture just the physical take, action or punch line that got me. My mental Vines, of course, chart a trail through my own theatregoing, film, TV and video-viewing career. What are yours, and what do they say about you and the world in which you live?

further reading

Recommendations for further reading will depend upon the individual reader's interest; details for all sources can be found below. Good, accessible introductions to the thought and philosophy of humour can be found in John Morreall's *Comic Relief: A Comprehensive Philosophy of Humor* (2009) and Simon Critchley's *On Humour* (2002). More scientific approaches would include *Inside Jokes: Using Humor to Reverse-Engineer the Mind* (2011), by Matthew M. Hurley, Daniel C. Dennett and Reginald B. Adams, Jr., with Robert R. Provine's *Laughter: A Scientific Investigation* written in refreshingly non-scientific terms. For ways into comedy as a genre, try *Comedy* (2004), by Andrew Stott, which has recently been given a second edition (2014); and my *Cambridge Introduction to Comedy* (2009).

Als, Hilton. 'Underhanded: Martin McDonagh's Slap in the Face'. *The New Yorker*, 15 March 2010. http://www.newyorker.com/magazine/2010/03/15/underhanded (accessed 12 September 2014).

Aristotle. *Poetics*, trans. Malcolm Heath. Harmondsworth: Penguin, 1996.

Attardo, Salvatore. *Linguistic Theories of Humor*. Berlin: Mouton de Gruyter, 1994.

————. 'A Primer for the Linguistics of Humor'. *The Primer of Humor Research*, ed. Victor Raskin. Berlin: Mouton de Gruyter, 2008. 101–56.

Attardo, Salvatore and Victor Raskin. 'Script theory revis(it)ed: joke similarity and joke representation model'. *Humor*. 4. 3/4. 1991. 293–347.

Barnes, Peter. 'Laughter!' *Barnes Plays: One*. London: Methuen, 1989. 339–411.

Bean, Richard. *One Man, Two Guv'nors*. London: Oberon, 2011. (Show clips: http://www.youtube.com/watch?v=0F_faR2yCeU. Accessed 26 December 2011.)

Beckett, Samuel. *Waiting for Godot. Samuel Beckett: The Complete Dramatic Works*. London: Faber and Faber, 1990. 7–88.

Berger, Peter L. *Redeeming Laughter: The Comic Dimension of Human Experience*. Berlin: Walter de Gruyter, 1997.

Bergson, Henri. 'Laughter'. *Comedy*, ed. Wylie Sypher. Baltimore: Johns Hopkins University, 1980. 59–190.

Bevis, Richard W. *The Laughing Tradition: Stage Comedy in Garrick's Day*. Athens: University of Georgia, 1980.

Billig, Michael. *Laughter and Ridicule: Towards a Social Critique of Humour*. London: Sage, 2010.

Brecht, Bertolt. 'The Street Scene: A Basic Model for an Epic Theatre'. *Brecht on Theatre: The Development of an Aesthetic*, ed. and trans. John Willett. London: Methuen, 1993. 121–9.

Brook, Peter. *The Empty Space*. New York: Touchstone, 1995.

Chafe, Wallace. *The Importance of Not Being Earnest*. Amsterdam: John Benjamins, 2009.

Critchley, Simon. *On Humour*. London: Routledge, 2002.

Davis, Jessica Milner. *Farce*. New Brunswick: Transaction, 2003.

Dillon, Matthew. 'Tragic Laughter'. *The Classical World*, 84.5, 1991. 345–55.

Döring, Tobias. 'Freud about Laughter – Laughter about Freud'. *A History of English Laughter: Laughter from Beowulf to Beckett and Beyond*, ed. Manfred Pfister. Amsterdam: Rodopi, 2002. 121–35.

Douglas, Mary. 'The Social Control of Cognition: Some Factors in Joke Perception'. *Man*, 3.3, September 1968. 361–76.

Freud, Sigmund. 'Humour'. *Art and Literature*, ed. Albert Dickson. Harmondsworth: Penguin, 1990 [1927]. 425–33.

Gerbert, Elaine. 'Laughing Priests in the Atsuta Shrine Festival'. *Humour and Religion: Challenges and Ambiguities*, eds. Hans Geybels and Walter Van Herck. London: Continuum, 2011. 54–65.

Gervais, Matthew, and David Sloan Wilson. 'The Evolution and Functions of Laughter and Humor: A Synthetic Approach'. *The Quarterly Review of Biology*, 80.4, December 2005. 395–430.

Ghose, Indira. 'Licence to Laugh: Festive Laughter'. *Twelfth Night. A History of English Laughter: Laughter from Beowulf to Beckett and Beyond*, ed. Manfred Pfister. Amsterdam: Rodopi, 2002. 35–46.

————. *Shakespeare and Laughter: A Cultural History*. Manchester: Manchester University, 2008.

Gibbs, James. *Wole Soyinka*. New York: Grove, 1986.

Gilhus, Ingvild Sælid. *Laughing Gods, Weeping Virgins: Laughter in the History of Religion*. New York: Routledge, 1997.

Goffman, Erving. *Frame Analysis: An Essay on the Organization of Experience*. Boston: Northeastern, 1986 [1974].

Gray, Frances. *Women and Laughter*. London: Macmillan, 1994.

Gregory, Lady Augusta. 'Spreading the News'. *Selected Writings*, ed. with an introduction by Lucy McDiarmid and Maureen Waters. London: Penguin, 1995. 312–28.

Griffiths, Trevor. *Comedians*. London: Faber and Faber, 1979.

Halliwell, Stephen. *Greek Laughter: A Study of Cultural Psychology from Homer to Early Christianity*. Cambridge: Cambridge University, 2008.

Holland, Norman. *Laughing: A Psychology of Humor*. Ithaca: Cornell University, 1982.

Hurley, Erin. *Theatre & Feeling*. Basingstoke: Palgrave Macmillan, 2010.

Hurley, Matthew M., Daniel C. Dennett, and Reginald B. Adams, Jr. *Inside Jokes: Using Humor to Reverse-Engineer the Mind*. Cambridge: MIT, 2011.

Hyers, Conrad. *The Laughing Buddha: Zen and the Comic Spirit*. Eugene: Wipf and Stock, 1989.

Limon, John. *Stand-Up Comedy in Theory, or, Abjection in America*. Durham: Duke University, 2000.

Louis, C. K. http://www.youtube.com/watch?v=6CmzT4OV-w0. Accessed 18 March 2013.

McCafferty, Owen. *Death of a Comedian*. London: Faber and Faber, 2015.

McGuinness, Frank. 'Carthaginians'. *Plays: 1*. London: Faber and Faber, 1996 [1988]. 291–379.

Meredith, George. 'An Essay on Comedy'. *Comedy*, ed. Wylie Sypher. Baltimore: Johns Hopkins University, 1980. 3–57.

Morreall, John, ed. *The Philosophy of Laughter and Humor*. Albany: State University of New York, 1987.

———. *Comic Relief: A Comprehensive Philosophy of Humor*. Chichester: Wiley-Blackwell, 2009.

———. 'Comic Vices and Comic Virtues'. *Humor*, 23.1, 2010. 1–26.

Murphy, Tom. *Bailegangaire*. *Murphy Plays: Two*. London: Methuen, 1993a. 89–170.

———. *A Thief of a Christmas*. *Murphy Plays: Two*. London: Methuen, 1993b. 171–242.

Nelson, Judith Kay. *What Made Freud Laugh: An Attachment Perspective on Laughter*. New York: Routledge, 2012.

Panksepp, Jaak. 'The Riddle of Laughter: Neural and Psychoevolutionary Underpinnings of Joy'. *Current Directions in Psychological Science*, 9.6, 2000. 183–6.

Panti. https://www.youtube.com/watch?v=WXayhUzWnl0. Accessed 23 July 2014.

Pfister, Manfred. 'Introduction: A History of English Laughter?' *A History of English Laughter: Laughter from Beowulf to Beckett and Beyond*, ed. Manfred Pfister. Amsterdam: Rodopi, 2002. v–x.

———. 'Beckett, Barker, and Other Grim Laughers'. *A History of English Laughter: Laughter from Beowulf to Beckett and Beyond*, ed. Manfred Pfister. Amsterdam: Rodopi, 2002. 175–89.

Phillips, Adam. *On Kissing, Tickling and Being Bored: Psychoanalytic Essays on the Unexamined Life*. London: Faber and Faber, 1994.

Propp, Vladimir. *On the Comic and Laughter*, ed. and trans. Jean-Patrick Debbèche and Paul Perron. Toronto: University of Toronto, 2009.

Provine, Robert R. 'Laughter'. *American Scientist*, 84.1, January–February 1996. 38–45.

———. *Laughter: A Scientific Investigation*. Harmondsworth: Penguin, 2001.

————. 'Laughing, Tickling, and the Evolution of Speech and Self'. *Current Directions in Psychological Science*, 13.6, 2004. 215–8.

Pryor, Richard. http://www.youtube.com/watch?v=9t9bFFSlrCk. Accessed 19 March 2013.

Purdie, Susan. *Comedy: The Mastery of Discourse*. Toronto: University of Toronto, 1993.

Ruhl, Sarah. *The Clean House*. New York: Samuel French, 2007.

Schopenhauer, Arthur. Extract from *The World as Will and Idea*. *The Philosophy of Laughter and Humor*, ed. John Morreall. Albany: State University of New York, 1987. 51–64.

Shakespeare, William. *Hamlet*. Arden Shakespeare, 2005.

Soyinka, Wole. *The Trials of Brother Jero*. *Three Short Plays*. Oxford: Oxford University, 1994. 43–77.

States, Bert O. *Great Reckonings in Little Rooms: On the Phenomenology of Theater*. Berkeley: University of California, 1985.

Stoppard, Tom. *Rosencrantz and Guildenstern Are Dead*. London: Faber and Faber, 2000.

Stott, Andrew. *Comedy*. London: Routledge, 2004.

Sutton-Smith, Brian. *The Ambiguity of Play*. Cambridge: Harvard, 1997.

Synge, J. M. *The Well of the Saints*. *Synge: The Complete Plays*. London: Methuen, 1995. 131–71.

Tönnies, Merle. 'Laughter in Nineteenth-Century British Theatre: From Genial Blending to Harsh Distinctions'. *A History of English Laughter: Laughter from Beowulf to Beckett and Beyond*, ed. Manfred Pfister. Amsterdam: Rodopi, 2002. 99–119.

Treadwell, Sophie. *Machinal*. London: Nick Hern, 1993 [1928].

'Victoria Wood As Seen On TV Piecrust Players' https://www.youtube .com/watch?v=1qK80wVXZ9w accessed 6 June 2015.

Walsh, Fintan. 'Pride, Politics, and the Right to Perform'. *Theory on the Edge: Irish Studies and the Politics of Sexual Difference*, ed. Noreen Giffney and Mira Hird. Basingstoke: Palgrave Macmillan, 2013. 105–22.

————. 'Cyberactivism and the Emergence of #TeamPanti'. *Theatre Research International*, 40.1, 2014. 104–7.

Weitz, Eric. 'Failure as Success: On Clowns and Laughing Bodies'. *Performance Research: A Journal of the Performing Arts*, 17.1, 2012. 79–87.

White, E. B. 'Some Remarks on Humor'. *Essays of E. B. White*. New York: Harper and Row, 1979. 243–9. (Originally published as "Preface" to *A Subtreasury of American Humor*, eds. E. B. White and K. White, 1941.)

Wilshire, Bruce. *Role Playing and Identity: The Limits of Theatre as Metaphor*. Bloomington: Indiana University, 1982.

Wood, Victoria. 'Giving Notes'. *The Contemporary Monologue: Women,* eds. Earley, Michael and Philippa Keil. London: Methuen, 1995. 40–2.

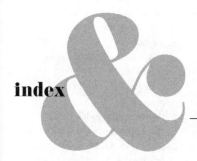

index

acknowledgements

During the course of this particular writing process I have been fortunate to receive various pieces of information, advice and support from a variety of people, including: Patrice Oppliger, Kunle Animashaun, Miren Somers, Fintan Walsh, Elaine Gerbert, the Tyrone Guthrie Centre and everybody there who makes it a creative haven, Brian Singleton, Jen Harvie and Dan Rebellato, Jenni Burnell, Lucy Knight – and the usual suspects: my parents, Eamonn, Liam, Benny and Ann.